MY SOCIOPATH

An Empath's Soul Journey Among Sociopaths

by

Lynna Kivela

First Published 2015 as a Kindle Direct Publishing ebook
Paperback Published, First Edition, 2015
Second Edition: Paperback and ebook 2016
ISBN-13: 978-1533661913
ISBN-10: 153366191X

Dedicated To Those On A Healing Path

&

For Michael

May We All Be On A Soul Journey

PREFACE

My Sociopath

This is my autobiographical tale that waivers along, sideways and oftentimes backwards on my path of Sociopath Awareness and trying to not only heal myself, but to gather enlightenment along the way. Henceforth, my personal journey of not only learning about myself and where I came from, but also of learning about those I attract. I was forcing myself to evolve through my writings to you; herein lies my offerings.

I do not rely much on the repeated words surrounding Narcissist Education and Healing but expand out and beyond what is often already expressed. I use my own experiences as patterns to be dissected and pieced back together in what makes logical sense to me. This book was an exercise in accessing Universal Knowledge or the concept of everything we need to know is inside us.

My greatest problem in writing was with the main terminology of the subject: Sociopath, Narcissist, and Borderline. All these disorders can look similar in their manifestation but are different in their primary impulses. I most often defaulted to the word *Narcissist* because it is the most general term for destructive behavior manifested through manipulation and control. In addition, since all Sociopaths are Narcissists and most Borderlines have Narcissism, *Narcissist* was the most expansive term. I use *Sociopath* when giving examples of the things My Sociopath did.

I use *he* to describe the personality disordered for simplicity of writing and these are my experiences. In my life travels, I've met many disruptive and horrible women. I believe this is largely due to the broken family-unit, the preoccupation with materialism, the obsession with social-media attention and stimulation, the manic pursuit of staying youthful in appearance, the need for sexual attention, and refusing to accept one's age and the wisdom and maturity that results from the natural growth and evolution in our life-span. Women are now acting like men and this is a detriment to our species. The female spirit is powerful, beautiful and needed for the evolution and healing of people and the planet.

I have concerns with so-called narcissist *experts* in the field of psychology who are writing articles and/or books: *Experts* claim that 1-4% of the population are narcissists (sociopaths). How can anyone determine how many narcissists are walking amongst us? Narcissists are covert and many go a lifetime creating chaos and misery and never end up in jail. And most people who are adversely affected by one, don't even know what hit them, and may live their lives cycling in and out of depression and blaming themselves for everything that seems to go wrong in their lives. When I was with My Sociopath and Turk Narc, they so expertly twisted my environment that I thought I was the crazy one. This is what Narcissists do. If a Narcissist does end up in counseling, he presents an illusion revolving around benign issues and effectively hides his malignancy in harming others.

Narcissism is deception behind well-executed and maneuvered manipulations, half-truths and lies. The result is the exploitation of the naïve, innocent, and weakened (temporary or permanent) for personal gain in one or more of the areas involving money, sex, power, prestige, attention, admiration or care-taking.

People are objects to be used by The Narcissist: Nothing more, nothing less.

- **Narcissists: Exploit Others**

- **Apaths: Eat, Sleep, and Reproduce**

- **Empaths: Restore Equilibrium**

The earth is just a dark reflection of the astral ocean, a reflection that shows everything upside down. What seems bad is good and what seems good is bad (Szepes, 96).

Table of Contents

Part One...Who Are They?

ONE

THEY ALL LOOK SO MUCH ALIKE

We Emotionally React To The Sociopath's Chilling Coldness

You are a constant emotional wreck full of reactions when with The Sociopath. Your emotional hurts are due to the fact that your trusting nature *cannot comprehend the eerie coldness, or lack of feelings and emotions coming from The Sociopath. Sociopaths are entities that look human, and we believe in their humanness when they love-bomb us (made our lives hopeful, perfect and exciting), and then we are suddenly face-to-face with vacantness, a monster...our nervous system goes into reaction mode. You do not know about Sociopaths and even if you did, this unfeeling coldness, lack of care and regard, is unfathomable to a normal human being who has emotions.*

You catch him in a lie and you expect him to cry or break-down, you expect him to try to explain, to talk, to apologize through a shaky, concerned and self-conscious voice...Normal human beings become upset and overly talkative when trying to explain their wrong or hurtful actions...

Yet, he remains cold, silent, aloof, detached, unfeeling, uncaring. He doesn't say a word; no communication. He just stares at you...Indifferent; nothing is inside of him; he is gone. He doesn't have to explain anything...you are the problem. If you keep on pressing, he will deny his lie with a few words: "That didn't happen." As simple as that; nothing more.

Though you caught him red-handed, he will calmly dismiss FACTS...of what was before your eyes: What you saw, what you know was there. He takes away REALITY. You go into shock because you are in another dimension...a LOW dimension...and you are in a zone of helplessness...he's coldly lying, denying, dismissing...you are in an emotional frenzy of being tossed into a world that doesn't exist for feeling and caring humans. He does NOT respond normally to human situations.

A common scenario: Since Sociopaths are fixated with catching the attention of those who will admire and look up to them, and they mostly crave the sexual component in these admirers and are driven to obsessive flirting: You catch him with another woman...you call him out on it. He will first deny that they were together...though you saw it! He boldly and assuredly denies truth. He obstinately calls her his "good friend" and you are made into the "insecure and jealous." He just flipped reality on you. How do you defend yourself? You are a horrible person that cannot deal with his female "friends."

He has a constant and rotating herd of female "friends" surrounding him; they are his ego-sources; there to make him feel good about himself, ease his boredom, act as backup targets in case he finds himself alone; or, they are there to support him and tell him how great he is when he destroys another intimate partner. The members of his herd also use him for their entertainment and to escape their own loneliness and boredom.

But wait, didn't he first deny he was even with this other woman? Sociopaths create such chaos in relationships, in their environment, that everything is lost in the fog. A Sociopath will twist and turn reality in such a scary way that our rational brain goes into hay-wire mode and we are left emotionally scrambling around in shock. They believe that they don't have to be accountable for anything!

Sociopaths are developmentally delayed as children where life is supposed to be ALL fun and play without responsibility. This is why they continually seek new relationships...They want to only experience the FUN part and never be responsible for The Work...The Responsibility, The Loyalty, The Trustworthiness...The Focus, Endurance and Steadfastness...what REAL relationships are. Sociopaths never invest in anything for long. When he is held accountable he will have a tantrum...overt, physical and aggressive; or, cold, shunning, and detached.

Sociopaths either take away our reality or they twist reality before our very eyes. They refuse to deal with real life in real ways. They even believe they are better than that! Yet, we were accountable for everything while with him! Sociopaths only seek out the loyal and dedicated; these are the people that tolerate their lack of responsibility, dependability, integrity and realness for the longest.

Not only is a Sociopath NEVER ACCOUNTABLE and NEVER RESPONSIBLE, but you are now the Bad One that demands it in your relationship, in your surroundings, and for your own safety.

The Sociopath remains cold and unemotional throughout this play...even more cold and unfeeling as the chaos accelerates! They are not saying a word...but remaining quiet.

They have taken us into a Non-human realm and we are spiraling downward as they are ascending upward. They become more cold and more emotionally detached as they witness our devastated reactions. This is their Time to Shine. They are the strong and stoic and we are the defective and weakened!

We might force an "apology" out of him...but Sociopaths repeat human words without true feelings behind them. They also do this when they say the "love" word to us. He only feels his version of "love" when he is having sex with a fresh target that admires him without question, without truly knowing him and before real-life happens...the honeymoon period...LUST not love. Nothing but words with no meaning. Sociopaths are never sorry. In his eyes, he NEVER does anything wrong.

You are now in The Sociopath's world and he love-bombed you into being a part of it. You cannot turn around and safely escape. You are now *the emotionally out-of-control and he is the Great One that is a master of his emotions. He will even claim that he is more highly evolved than you, better than you...He is in control of his emotions, you are not.*

Sadly, some Sociopaths will use and exploit religious and spiritual teachings as a defense for their coldness, detachment, never admitting responsibility, and lack of ownership for the hurt they inflict and unwillingness to explain themselves: he is "taking the higher road" when you are wallowing in the "low road of emotionalism."

However, because they have damaged brains they do not realize the "higher road" is NOT taken after their inflicted Destruction. This is where The Sociopath is delusional and this is where we are emotionally reacting to his delusional world. Sociopaths get to do whatever they want, when they want, and therefore, they do not really cause harm (in their eyes). In his world, only your reaction to his destruction (that he didn't really do) is harmful! Twist on Reality. You will hear stories of many "screaming exes" out of the mouths of Sociopaths. They drive those who love them insane.

He will then tell everyone that it didn't work out with you because you were too emotional, or jealous, or controlling, or you had a bad childhood, or you are Bipolar or Crazy! The Smear-Campaign is in full force. Sociopaths love the "bipolar" word and use it to label ANYONE that is emotionally reacting to their bad behavior and unfair treatment. He remains the Victim Boy with his enablers and supporters...."Poor Man can never find love." Sociopaths leave a long trail of many destroyed relationships and it was never their fault; their supporters keep them strong by enabling their victim-hood.

The start of this scenario, or his cold and uncaring lies and denials, are forgotten...you are now upset and in his world of self-preservation, that is BAD. He does not have empathy for you because you are not feeding his ego. You are not allowed to question him on anything, nor judge him, nor ask him questions about his harmful behaviors toward you...You are ONLY allowed to passively and quietly accept him, feed his ego by telling him how great and good-looking he is, join him for intense activities, and give him sex when he needs it.

When you hold him accountable, he will seek a "fresh" ego-source to look adoringly into his eyes, smile up at him to make him feel "alive," and to feed his ego. She will soon find herself in this same hell-cycle; it doesn't take long before the "honeymoon infatuation" wears off.

Real human beings have EMOTIONS and we are driven "crazy" by the spine-chilling coldness, play and emotional unresponsiveness torture of A Sociopath...The Sociopath that we wrongly believed loved us. END

Sociopaths and Narcissists certainly don't resemble the black-hoodie wearing little guy with lowered head hiding behind a corner that we all see in the media. They look like us...actually, they look better than us. They have an energy about them that shouts to the world, "Come along and let's have a fun and exciting ride together." They have very high energy levels and the rest of us get absorbed into their spiraling vortex; they make us feel 'high.'

Sociopaths live in Disneyland and we are lured into their gates for a day of fun. He is the voice behind "It's a Small World" and we are hypnotized. He is the conductor of our childhood songs.

Though most personality disordered individuals have two or more conditions chiming along with one another, there are subtle distinctions between what disorder is playing out the strongest. Narcissism is a more refined and controlled version of Sociopathy and Borderline Personality Disorder (BPD). Narcissists are more systematic and less chaotic behaving than a Sociopath or Borderline. Narcissists are the best at keeping their inner-chaos hidden so it is not so apparent; they are covert in their destruction. Borderlines act wildly and destructively out-of-control, and hurt themselves as much as they hurt others, if not, more so; they are their own worst enemies. Sociopaths manifest behaviors between a Narcissist and Borderline: they are extremely manipulative, controlling, contriving, and destructive and at times (when under stress), cannot keep their chaos-creation hidden; they can have emotional breakdowns like the Borderline.

Sociopath

Use and manipulate others for their own needs and without conscience. These needs are financial, more comfortable living situation, sex, attention, improved social status, and care-taking or 'mothering.' The Sociopath craves new love and the associated honeymoon period of someone being enthralled, without question, by the image he presents. He is equally blind by love and sees no fault in his new target and only fantasizes how she will fill all his needs and emptiness.

A Sociopath has no ability for his own inner-fulfillment and must fill his soul void by an outer source that is reflecting new love and adoration upon him. He discards her once her resources dry up, or she starts questioning his lies, manipulations, and inconsistencies, so that he may quickly find someone new to fill his inner-abyss. Once he discards her, she is *dead* to him because he no longer feels pumped up with life by her. Just like many of us view our morning coffee grounds: Gave us a high, lifted us up, now soggy and wet, can't reuse, can't get another high from, throw away to start with fresh grounds that will re-stimulate us again. Sociopaths are constantly seeking stimulation. We all eventually become used coffee grounds to a sociopath. This is also represented in their hobby or interest jumping; they lose interest in everything...including themselves.

His stimulation comes from the illumination of your adoring and glowing face when you are utterly in awe and lust with him...actually you are not even enthralled by him but by the Love Mask he wears. A Sociopath has no identity; he is merely a master display of an image that pleases and acts to heighten the intrigue of the target that he is pursuing.

A Sociopath is cunning and deliberate in his methods to win over a new victim. He lies, tells half-truths, distorts facts and changes the timeline of events. He is the perpetual victim and you will feel sorry for him. If he abused, cheated on, and discarded his wife for a new target, and she later finds a new lover, he will change the timeline that she cheated on him first and that's why he discarded and left her; he had to. Yes, his ex eventually found a new lover but it was after he devalued her, devastated their living environment (financially and emotionally), and then cruelly left her. He tells this flip-version of events to his new target and she feels sad and immediately starts forming an emotional connection to him. Most women are instinctively mothering when it comes to what appears like a vulnerable and broken-down man.

When he is winning you over, or what is called the "Love-Bombing" stage, he is very controlled, deliberate, smooth, calm, and seems to echo all your wants, needs and desires. In the beginning, he listens to who you are, where you came from, where you are going, what interest you and what scares you. He becomes your hero. During love-bombing, he takes you on a wild ride of events that match what you love in life. If you are into yoga, he will one-up that and take you to a Flying-Yoga session where you are not only in your ecstasy, but you are viewing him, the initiator and creator of this event, as a dream come true upon wings.

He Is A Creator Of Events.

A Sociopath is a master at one-upping everything in your life that you formerly experienced to create exhilarating roller-coaster moments with you. Experiencing these extreme highs with The Sociopath during the initial love-bombing stage is addictive and you quickly fall in love with him. This is what he wants. He seems equally in love with you but in actuality, he is falling in "love" with himself. He keeps falling in love with himself with every smile and adoring reflection he gains from the target. **He is feeding off your strong attraction toward him; you are his ego-source fueling his desires for himself.** My Sociopath refers to the early stages of a new relationship as "It's Fresh." He is feeling "fresh" because he has not yet laid the framework for dread and despair. He has not yet sabotaged her environment...all's well because of Honeymoon Lust.

A Sociopath Seeks Constant Freshness.

I am dating Mr.Oh during the editing of this book. I'm being controlled and smart by maintaining my independence, staying focused on my growth and keeping clarity of thought. He is emotionally vulnerable, little sense-of-self mixed with moments of exaggerated sense-of-self, driven by exhilarating moments where his energy stimulates himself and others and then he sinks into despair and insecurity regarding his future wellness. I mentioned to him that he was a "Creator of Events." I didn't realize what a wonderful compliment this was so he now out-does each activity we do together from the previous. This is all well and good for my tired soul, but he is also creating Grand Events with everyone else that comes along. He obsesses over impressing large quantities of people, winning their approval, and when he and I find a special activity to do together, he forgets I am there and becomes possessed with thoughts of pulling other people into our time. He loses track of himself, and me, and enters into a world of neurotic texting and reaching out to people where his soul is emptied into visions of a delusional world of People and their Adoring and Approving Eyes. I am transformed out of my humanness and into his generic object of stimulation.

I must keep on a high mental plane with thoughts that understand his limitations and keep measured in my emotions...to not react to his chaotic energy field that he cast outward from his confused soul...evidence that he is lost in a universe that he cannot harmonize with. However, I know that I am physically and financially safe with him. He is extremely generous and wants nothing else but for me to play Tinker Bell to his Peter Pan. He wants a flickering fairy of fun. And because of the hashing out of My Sociopath in these writings and being goal oriented, I can harness his demands effectively by keeping time to myself and most of all, I can now be a strong gate-keeper for my emotional and mental health.

Sociopaths Love to be Loved. They Need to be Needed.

Those of us victimized by a Sociopath tend to think about them in either black or white, well, mostly black, and since Sociopaths have this limited thinking, we should not. Actually, there is gray when defining a Sociopath.

Our black thinking being that *Sociopaths are incapable of love.* **They do love.** However, it is felt during the fast-paced honeymoon period and at other times when someone is subjugating themselves over to his power and without imparting expectations or demands. He loves during the *fresh* stage of a relationship and it is emanating from his delusional mind: His Greatness, The Fresh or Subjugating Person's Greatness, Their Greatness Together and Two Greats Join Together to Have Great Sex and Great Adventures. Though this stage feels like real love for a Sociopath, and even many non-sociopaths, it is primarily LUST and infatuation. There have been many cases of marriages occurring during this lustful period and some have worked out, but of course, this is with somewhat healthy people. The difference being that people with adequately grounded personalities can transition their feelings of lust into compassion, commitment, dedication and loyalty. Sociopaths are not capable of this.

The honeymoon period is one of the few times they actually feel alive and capable of love. He is confident that the new target will always adore him and he is hopeful for their future. However, a Sociopath is an avoider of real-life so as soon as the honeymoon period ends, or she starts putting real responsibility on him, so does this great and everlasting love; he becomes bored and craves fresh adoration from a new people-source that will propel him into feeling that lust again; lust without strings. He is emotionally stuck as a little boy that only wants to play on the playground and not pick up his toys.

The typical honeymoon period lasts anywhere from a few weeks to a few months. She can extend this period longer but she would have to give him sex at his every beck and call, cook and clean constantly, make lots of money to help sustain his grandiose lifestyle, and admire and compliment him all day. A Histrionic woman would get along well with a Sociopath...she needs sexual attention and stimulation just as much as he does. However, when she turns excessively demanding or seeks attention from other sources, The Sociopath will breakdown. Another way to maintain a longer honeymoon period is to turn a blind eye to his constant flirting, attention seeking, and lack of dependability.

Sociopaths are love addicts!

Narcissist

Narcissists are similar to Sociopaths but are more controlled and can have fleeting moments of guilt and regret when things go wrong in their intimate relationships. However, these bad feelings are short-lived and will fly out the window when they manage to manipulate the target into returning, or if they immediately gain a new target. Narcissists are more charming and likable than Sociopaths and can acquire and maintain a group of supporters from a higher social and education class. Narcissists are not compelled to work hard or to be overly generous to win people over. They innately feel that their presence is sufficient enough to gain the attention they desire from others. A Narcissist has more ability to focus and to achieve goals thus placing him in higher professional positions and roles. This wanes as he gets older.

DIFFERENCE IN THE DETAILS

Schooling And Education

Narcissist: Can complete higher-level degrees such as a master's and beyond. They tend to focus on obtaining degrees while younger but this learning focus fizzles as they become older. They stop expanding when in a secured position. Their education focus is more on degrees where they can obtain a pedestal type of position or have power and radiate glamour over others: Professors, Attorneys, Judges. For example, a Professor (PhD) versus a Medical Doctor (MD): There is less ongoing work and study required after obtaining a PhD and tenureship than after obtaining an MD. A professor works fewer hours and has abundant more off-time than a doctor. Narcissists are lazy but they are smart and know what degrees to achieve that will mean the least amount of work with the most glamour. Add to this, a professor has hordes of young, glowing girls adoring him whereas a doctor is doing prostate exams on cranky, elderly men in small rooms. It is likely there are more narcissistic Professors than MD's (non-surgeons).

Sociopath: May be able to achieve a bachelor's degree while younger but it is a struggle. The Sociopath does not have the Narcissist's focus abilities. If a Sociopath does obtain any degree it will be a softer degree in the Liberal Arts, Social Sciences or in a certification program. Even at this, they will struggle. Not only do they have more chaotic brain-wiring than The Narcissist, but they will be more focused on the drama of fellow students, roommates and the professors and likely involved in much of the drama as well. Sociopaths also think they know more than the professors and innately feel a power struggle with the instructor out of extreme insecurity in not being able to control the classroom.

Exes, Family Members, Female Friends

Narcissist: Attempts to stay close to exes even after bad breakups. He manipulates the codependent ex to believe their ongoing "friendship" will benefit her. He believes in his own grandiosity and convinces her to remain in his life. Since he continually fed his exes (before they were exes) brainwashing images and details of his Grandiosity, she thoroughly believes there is no greater man and she easily falls into the *Narcissist-Ex-Remains-Friend* trap. She is primed. Most importantly, by making her into his "friend," he believes he is The Great One and at no fault in their previous tumultuous relationship. He believes if he were so bad, she wouldn't still be his "friend." He is redeemed.

Turk Narc believes his family and everyone sharing his blood is superior. Upon first becoming acquainted with Turk Narc, he told me of his grand Pasha relatives of the Great Ottoman Empire as we stared at old pictures of them hanging in a row, down the walls of his home, emanating the feel of a nervous museum. Turk Narc spoke of his mother as a Supreme Being. Narcissists have little respect for women besides their own mothers.

Every male and female "friend" that Turk Narc ever associated with were, according to him, the best quality human and came from the greatest "stock" and "bloodline." He was all about family background and if a great woman came from an *inferior* family then she was tarnished even though she proved her trustworthiness, loyalty, graciousness, workhorse abilities, intelligence, and fortitude beyond any other Great Stock Woman. Narcissists see superficial image only. They want people of prestige and title as part of their entourage; they are name and title droppers. Narcissists believe that merely being in their presence is a gift and this gift should only be bestowed upon the deserving.

You, who showed loyalty to The Narcissist, soon becomes defective and yet his random, female followers are pedestaled (as we were at one time too). We tolerated his constant entourage of superior "female friends;" they were always lurking around. We were brainwashed to believe that his female "groupies" were something that we should accept to be such a cool woman in such a cool man's life. Narcissists are easily bored and need constant energy or ego feeding from female "friends" who are also feeding him constant adoring looks, praise, admiration, and compliments. If these females were not feeding his ego with praise, they would not be female "friends." I put "friends" in quotes because he is either hoping and planning to, or actually having sex with one or more of these females. He keeps these female "friends" attached and lingering as potential and future sources of supply.

Sociopath: More hatred and destruction toward intimate partners/family members and when The Devalue starts, he will burn bridges. Sociopaths don't pedestal family members as much as Narcissists do; especially in the delusional mindset of Mother as Supreme Being. Sociopaths have more hatred and bitterness toward their mothers, siblings and friends.

My Sociopath hated his father and discarded him but when his father went to his death bed, My Sociopath became his ultimate caretaker. When a Sociopath is a caretaker he is in complete control of the other person; the weakened person is in a dependent condition and that is when a Sociopath thrives in the 'relationship.' He fumed when he told me that his sister received a banana from their father when they were young and he did not. Fifty-years later he tells me this "banana story" as if it just happened. He spit venom as he spread rumors that his sister deserved her breast cancer and she cheated her way through advanced degrees. He sought out his sister's ex husband to tell him the same and they both sat stewing in poison. His sister is his greatest enabler and helped him take down many of a good woman. If she were to succumb to her breast cancer, he would stand gloriously by her side and be her savior.

Sociopaths have lower standards for their female groupies. He wants females around him that are less intelligent and inferior in circumstances to him. A woman who lacks self-esteem will cater to him and give him more grunt work. Sociopaths don't care what education or class-level his supporters are; just as long as they look up to him. He strives for quantity of enablers, not necessarily quality or title. His female "friends" are more of the outcast females that enable him because they believe in his male superiority and strength and consider him a protective daddy-figure in their lonely lives. He is insecure around male figures who are not his supporters and this means that his female enablers should not bring around male competition. He is like a tomcat and competing males diminish his appearance of ultimate power.

Sociopaths have creepier auras and their enablers are more mentally weak.

Appearance

Narcissist: Fits stereotypical image of a person preoccupied with physical appearance and constantly pursuing the fountain of youth: a young, pig-tailed girl gazing at herself in a reflective pond or a physically fit man staring at his muscles in the mirror. Narcissists have more solid belief systems regarding nutrition and exercise as it relates to health and anti-aging. Turk Narc obsesses over the latest anti-aging research to prevent or slow down cellular death and he's had invasive cosmetic procedures since his 40s. He seeks out miracle creams, foods, herbs and spices. Narcissists thrive in the current times of abundant gyms, health food stores and easily accessible organic vegetables, herbal remedies and supplements. They are very tuned into their looks and the ravishes of time. Their youth must remain in tack for as long as possible to attract the young girls (young boys) and to stay the center of attention...the life of the party.

Turk Narc and I reunited, again, after a separation that lasted many years. It was my birthday and during our separation I discovered an interesting Italian restaurant. It had cracked cement floors painted in earthy brown colors and I felt as if I were entering the Tuscany countryside. I thought Turk Narc would not only appreciate this but their eggplant dish as well. Turks take pride in their fifty-two ways to prepare eggplant and we both loved interesting and unusual dishes. I asked if we could go to this Italian restaurant for my birthday. Turk Narc was cheap and never spent a lot of money or thought on my birthday: it was always a last minute consideration. Not only was I conditioned from childhood to not speak up for myself but I stayed conditioned to expect, to want, to ask for little from Turk Narc (the Good Empath that I am): *Just buy me dinner at a special place I found.* I was proud for making such a unique discovery and relished in finally measure up to the Grand Turk; I was finally an intellectual discoverer of great cuisine. I felt good about myself...for a moment.

This birthday at My Discovery Place meant a lot to me and plus I was back with Turk Narc. Upon entering, The Turk became morose and turned into a zombie. He wasn't impressed. I excitedly explained the great eggplant dish: *It was made of thin layers, not thick like traditionally prepared.* The Zombie scowled and grimaced over the menu. The waiter came and I excitedly ordered the eggplant...Zombie was obsessed with his skin's elasticity and wanted calamari, but NOT breaded and fried, because anything fried broke down skin elasticity and screwed up collagen rebuilding properties. The calamari had to be sauteed in garlic and olive oil. Zombie needed to stay youthful to appeal to the young girls at his college. Unlike A Sociopath, Turk Narc saw his own aging process. He went over and over this special calamari request until the broken down waiter agreed that it could be managed in the kitchen. My hope that I would finally share something special with Turk Narc was destroyed and as in my childhood, I had no birthday celebration.

His sauteed calamari arrived and *it was rubbery and awful*; well, of course, squid is rubbery by nature. I didn't feel the same about my special eggplant dinner that lie in front of me; Turk Narc dismissed it too with a dirty look. The People-Pleaser in me wallowed in agony as I begged him to try a piece of eggplant so that I could get back my former excitement. He tried it with corners of mouth turned into downward hooks and swallowed with a tortured grimace.

Narcissists have stronger and more solidified belief systems that veer less than Sociopaths when seeking a new target or with an established target; they are sure of their superiority and feel confident that the new target will follow along with their identity. If the potential target does not conform to him, she will not be turned into his intimate partner. Plus, he believes he only deserves the best of everything, including food. Narcissists are spoiled brats.

I am grateful that I am able to eat each day, multiple times a day, and have access to decent quality food, because there are so many people and animals starving in this world. When I was divorcing My Sociopath, I was grateful to have a couple of eggs for dinner and a safe roof over my head. Empaths can think in these broad ways; we are tuned into the suffering of the world. Narcissists are very narrow and confined thinkers; they are not tuned in to anything besides their selfish needs.

Sociopath: Are not as concerned with their appearance and deny their own shortcomings; they disconnect from the reality of what they look like. He does not put emphasis on a healthy diet and exercise. A short, fat and bald Sociopath is self-confident in pursuing a good-looking catch. He compensates with generosity, humor, his material image and surroundings, and pulling off exciting activities. This works for the less attractive Sociopath because he comes across unsuspecting and safe.

(More in Chapter 2: *Physical Appearance*)

Generosity

Narcissist: Cheap gifts and no thought to gift giving toward others and especially intimate partners. However, they expect the best gifts from everyone else. Everything is a last-minute rush and little regard or consideration of the event, or the politeness required.

Does not always care about portraying an image of generosity; they believe their presence alone is generous enough. They are not as over-the-top generous when winning over a new admirer as The Sociopath is.

Selfish hoarders of their property and money and are smarter with finances than The Sociopath.

Sociopath: Has lower self-esteem than The Narcissist so he must work harder to impress. More generous when it comes to winning over a new target or picking up tabs to gain influence and admiration of supporters. He is also generous in gift-giving when he is trying to get or stay in close rapport to a new or past target's family.

A Sociopath will only be generous when he thinks it will benefit him in the gaining of "social currency" (enablers, supporters, waiting targets). Just like The Narcissist, social activities are a last-minute consideration but a Sociopath will spend more money even though it is in a quick, thoughtless, last-minute and frantic way.

Shares more of his money and property with a new target in the beginning but once he wins her over, he is more severe in excluding her from his resources. Generosity is not needed with a controlled target.

Sociopaths have more extremes in their behaviors than do Narcissists. Narcissists are more steady and consistent in their selfishness.

<u>*Sleep*</u>

Narcissist: Very peaceful, sound sleepers. Again, this goes back to seeking the fountain-of-youth. Narcissists need their sleep for their beautification. Rest and sleep is an inward process and Narcissists are better at this than Sociopaths.

Narcissists are not as worried about missing out on chances for controlling or manipulating someone to their favor on facebook, other social media or in their immediate surroundings (e.g., texting) because they believe that everyone loves and admires them anyway and those who don't, are only missing out.

Sociopath: Poor quality and not enough sleep. I believe this makes their manifested chaos and emotional problems worse. A Sociopath's inability to get a long duration of solid sleep connects to their problems with effective thinking and sound decision-making. Sociopaths are much more emotionally and behaviorally out-of-control than Narcissists. But what came first: their chaotic brain miswiring and misfiring, therefore, lack of good sleep, or, lack of good sleep that creates more chaotic and brain misfiring or more extreme Sociopathy? These two factors feed into and off one another. The sleep-cycles of the personality disordered require more study.

Can't Turn off their Minds Searching for Completeness: Mere Images on Social Media fulfill their Ideal

My Sociopath rarely slept. He trolled the internet all night admiring the images of women that he instantly concluded were The Ideal. Sociopaths inflate the external representations of images to an ideal level not realizing there is a difference between an image and reality; they live in a delusional fantasy-land. They are in a constant state of Idealizing most any potential ego-source that they believe will fill their empty internal-void and be their "mother."

They not only want "mothers" but they want these "mothers" to be their "daughters." They want a "little girl" to be dependent upon "Big Daddy" and yet they want little girl to be Mothering Spirit and Caretaker as well.

My Sociopath couldn't stop tracking images on the internet. Young girls, as well as older women, filled his delusional mind with a hope that anyone of these superficial images could be his completeness. Sociopaths have a hard time turning off their mind's preoccupation with finding wholeness in the images that surround them in their everyday or online life. They cannot shut down their brains for a peaceful sleep ... they might miss something ... someone!

Sociopaths cannot sleep because it is death to them. They are lost souls and need people, places and activities to feel alive. Sociopaths cannot access their soul to use this energy to radiate into their personalities. Instead, they need and use our personalities for their energy. They must stay awake for superficial and external human sources of attention that may come along to act as a spark to radiate their personality; they CANNOT miss any opportunity! They are like children who cannot go to sleep on Christmas Eve from fear of missing Santa Claus and his gifts.

Future Marriages And More Children

Narcissist: Less likely to remarry and to have children when older. He is better at delayed gratification and more able to learn from previous lessons. The Narcissist feels the accumulated emotional and financial stresses that he suffered from his many destroyed relationships and wants to live selfishly in his later years.

Sociopath: Wants to live free and careless as well but has no ability to practice delayed gratification or to learn from previous lessons. He is a breeder and seeks the quick "high" of impregnating a new target.

A Sociopath will quickly claim a woman, most any woman who is succumbing to his power, and "knock her up." Animal urges drive him and the phrase "knock her up" is appropriate because this gratifies him, in the animal sense, to "plant a seed" within her. He feels alive, manly, in power, and in "love" (actually, more in love with the power of his sperm, but he does not recognize this) when he impregnates. His prey is now forever tethered to him and for a moment in time, he feels contently satiated and settled within himself.

Older Sociopaths are known to inappropriately have children way too late in life and immediately into a new relationship with a new target. This is to get that impregnating "love" rush, to permanently claim the new target, and to show-off to supporters and former targets that she is not only "flowing with milk and honey," but he is "loved" by this Fertile, Young Goddess and therefore, he is Desired Virile Man. He will loudly broadcast this new "love," in an immature and show-off way, to prove he is The Good One, The Right One.

Sociopaths do not operate mentally and with intelligence; they are not thinkers and planners; they operate emotionally and from animal instincts. His other children, from various other mothers, may hate him because of his cold disregard, selfish behaviors, and how he destroyed and tossed them aside to start a new family, but these facts will not penetrate or alter his future behaviors and he will still continue to make new families. Nothing registers with a Sociopath! Even more alarming: His enablers will congratulate him on this manifested sickness of his serial family and baby-making and not regard the looming dangers for the new mother and child.

Borderline Personality Disorder

Borderlines are highly reactive, emotional roller-coasters and uncontrolled in their destruction. Many Narcissists are Borderlines and since all Sociopaths are Narcissists, there is a great amount of overlapping traits of these personality disorders. Primary characteristics are the key factor.

The word Unbalanced describes Borderline Personalities in completeness. He has the same high energy of The Socio/Narc and ability to capture intense love interests in moving targets, but his relationships are more drama filled and shorter lived and the honeymoon period ends much quicker and more dramatically.

He turns on you at the slightest hint of real life or responsibility. You and the relationship will transform into one of him loving and hating you day by day. Borderlines want and demand everything from you, attention beyond your 100%, and feel dejected at the slightest hint where his ego is put into question. He will then have a rage attack or psychologically torture you with silence and a physical withdraw and ultimately, and in an instant, emotionally disconnect from you.

Everything with a Borderline is more intense, moment by moment and abrupt than with a Socio/Narc. He is more likely to do the cruel silent-treatment.

To him, everything is either a pumping up or an insult, hurt and rejection to his ego; there is no ego moderation or control. He thrives from smiles, approvals and compliments and dies from disapprovals and judgments. Borderlines have the lowest self-esteem as compared to The Sociopath or Narcissist.

Borderlines swing from being overtly physically violent or aggressive to appearing calm but covertly employing manipulative and psychological moves against their opponent (loved ones). The violent episodes are sometimes alcohol or drug related; he may physically beat you as well as destroy your property and steal your belongings. He will have moments of recognition regarding his wrong acts but will blame it on an addiction or an emotional problem such as depression or being bipolar. In actuality, he does damaging things to you because he feels you disrespected or rejected him and deserve it. With arrogance and righteousness, Borderlines will tell you one story and play out another in your relationship. He will turn on you at any mention of accountability and view you as a *Cruel, Abusing Authority Figure.* Whereas The Sociopath or Narcissist portrays those who oppose him as *Crazy or Bipolar.*

Borderlines use being *depressed* or *bipolar* as an excuse for their bad behavior, whereas The Socio/Narc accuse those that oppose him as being *bipolar.* I am alert to anyone that throws around this overused and misunderstood label.

People with Borderline have a better moral understanding than a Socio/Narc but they allow wild emotional swings and addictions to take control and veer themselves off a more productive path in life. They live and act on impulse and self-sabotage their lives. They leap through hobbies, interests, courses of studies even quicker than The Sociopath (narcissists have the longest staying power)...losing interest quickly and seldom completing anything. Their relationships with people are no different. Invest wild and extreme gestures and intense emotions into one person and the moment a new face shows up, drop the original person in an instant. Borderlines give up on everything and everyone; they give up on themselves. They want to reform but can't and internally struggle. On the other hand, a Socio/Narc has little regard for his reform and will only feign regret when he needs someone or something.

Those with BPD show the most intense emotions with regard to their sense of self-entitlement. Therefore, they are the least emotionally attuned to the problems of others. They have the most heightened sense of emotionalism regarding their own issues and the most emotionally vacant regarding the issues of others. They are the ones that will turn and run at the slightest hint of someone's distress or need. However, they will reappear after the crisis, and do a Grand Gesture. He won't be there when you are sick but he will buy you the most beautiful and expensive flowers for your funeral. He is the greatest Fair Weather Friend.

Borderlines experience the deepest lows and highest highs; they may contemplate suicide. They don't have the unwavering belief in the power of their physical manifestation (body) to expertly manipulate and manage their physical surroundings and all the people in it. They don't believe they are the Master Chess Piece Mover like The Socio/Narc. Contrary to this, a Socio/Narc thinks too highly of himself and believes that his presence is significant in the scheme of his immediate surroundings.

According to "I Hate You, Don't Leave Me," A Borderline suffers from a kind of 'emotional hemophilia'; she lacks the clotting mechanism needed to moderate her spurts of feeling. Prick the delicate 'skin' of a borderline, and she will emotionally bleed to death (p. 12).

The Emotional Vampire

An Emotional Vampire depletes your energy within moments of an interaction and you walk away feeling bad about yourself. You become absorbed in the process of their taking you emotionally and psychologically down. You can't walk away from their energy that has penetrated both your inner-dwelling place and your outer being. An Emotional Vampire penetrates your boundaries, actually your weak or even lack of boundaries, and says such inappropriate things to you in a way that dominates and freezes your response system. You become a startled and frozen animal that sees the evil hunter's gun barrel pointing down upon you but you are numb and cannot defend or protect yourself; you have a hard time walking away.

An Emotional Vampire will exclaim "You look so tired!" to make you feel insecure, whereas a Narcissist will say, "You're the most beautiful thing I've ever seen" to win you over.

Open People (empaths) are kind, old souls and not only do the undeveloped or young souls detect us, but they feel comfortable dumping their darkness upon us; they know we will absorb it. There is a woman at work that I try to avoid but somehow I always get caught in her web. Each time this woman sees me she remarks that I look sick, am too white and I need to tan more. I repeatedly inform her of my Finnish ancestry and have to explain we are not tanning people. I find myself excusing away my Finnishness.

Here are some things that I've experienced with My Emotional Vampire at Work:

1. Critiquing and obsessing over my physical appearance:

You look tired. Are you sick? Have you gained weight?

2. Fishing for compliments of her appearance:

She has successfully critiqued and criticized my looks and I am ready to make an escape with the excuse of a made-up appointment. She quickly turns the focus to herself. She becomes self-deprecating; pulling at her skin and saying *Look at my wrinkles*; jiggling her hips and exclaiming *I'm so fat*; constantly mentioning her age and saying *I'm so old*. I am absorbed by these antics and feel compelled to compliment The Emotional Vampire. Actually, any person would be cornered into complimenting; there's no other exit from this show.

I stand there as a drained and depleted Empath that was seconds away from an escape with a shred of self-esteem and now I cannot move; she turns from the hunter to the injured animal with an *old face* and *fat body*. I let go of my emotional injuries and recent idea of escape and I succumb to being absorbed by My Emotional Vampire. I realize that I really do have to get going or else I will be late in doing what I was supposed to be doing to improve my life, but instead stay to compliment her looks.

She stands in her Transforming Emotional Vampire self: from dominating, preaching, slaughtering down with disguised cruelty in the form of knowing what's best for my health and wellness, to condemning me and everyone else to their inevitable after-life burning in hell, to that of a crumbling down and aging woman who is sad and miserable. I now come to the rescue of the person that just tore me down.

3. Zealot and Rigid Thinking:

Very narrow and confined belief system; forceful preaching to most anyone, especially Empaths, because we are more likely to tolerate it. Every other religion or spirituality is wrong and evil and everyone else is bound to hell....except My Emotional Vampire, of course. But when she preaches her religious dogma, an eerie cloud of evil manifests in her aura.

4. **Expert on Every Subject:**

   I have degrees in Special Education and if we start discussing Autism, for example, My Emotional Vampire knows more on this subject than I do. Emotional Vampires do not acknowledge or respect another person's knowledge, expertise, field of work and/or study and will not listen. They slam down and conversationally conquer someone more educated in the field in which the discussion is based.

5. **Always one class, one test, one small obstacle away from numerous degrees/certificates**

6. **Litigious**:

   Just like they suck the energy out of us, they suck the energy out of court systems by filing numerous lawsuits.

I just spent two-hours being led around by My Emotional Vampire into emotional depletion and dread...I did nothing but yet when I'm finally slaughtered and immobile, I decide to make an escape with the last fumes of my embarrassing and wrongly lived life out to the parking lot. My Emotional Vampire follows me and tells me a dreadful tale of her life situation. I stand near my car, telling her everything will be okay, with one hand on my door handle, as I allow my Finnish skin to burn.

(During the writing of this book, Randy, my friend at work, killed himself. About a year ago, Randy approached me to say "hello" as My Emotional Vampire was absorbing me. She was mean and rude to him; he slunked away. I was shocked by her behavior and apologized to Randy for her actions. Emotional Vampires need to put all their focus and attention into absorbing one person at a time and get easily irritated if other people interrupt this process. It is something to consider: How many people quietly kill themselves because of the tormenting effects of living in a world with unthinking and unevolved souls?)

All these personality disorders dance alongside one another.

People with personality disorders are increasing in numbers as our world turns more stressful and chaotic. We're all lost souls without roles. The seeking of instant gratification, attention and external stimulation is obsessive.

Vertical vs. Horizontal Summary of Personality Disorders:

♦ Sociopaths, Narcissists, Borderlines and Emotional Vampires see not only themselves, but everything and everyone on The Vertical...a Ladder.

♦ Sociopaths and Narcissists see people above and below them. They claw at to overcome those above them and kick at to keep those below them down.

♦ Borderlines and Emotional Vampires also live on The Vertical. However, they feel below everyone and must desperately grab up at and try to pull down those they feel are higher so that they can better *survive*.

♦ Healthy people live on The Horizontal where there is a sense of cooperation between everyone and in everything.

TWO

PHYSICAL APPEARANCE

Narcissists have an amazing way of exuding good looks and desirability though they are not necessarily endowed with these qualities. They believe, in their delusional minds, not only are they extraordinary specimens of human genetics, but so are their parents and their children. I have fallen in love with men that in no way resemble the prototypical handsome man, but because of my open heart toward love, I allow myself to be absorbed into his self-projected vortex of attractiveness and desirability. Narcissists are not always the best looking people and learn to compensate for this from an early age in other ways. Some of them may focus on building superior bodies, in pursuing powerful and dominant careers that exude maleness (attorneys, CEO's, stockbrokers) or in developing exciting and charming personalities.

Once a Narcissist builds a compensating feature to overshadow an unattractive one, he no longer sees his less than desirable asset(s) and becomes enamored by his own distracting shadow that he cast. He can be short, fat, bald or have an unattractive face but because he radiates such high-energy when on the prowl for a new target, or when nourishing his enablers, he believes himself to be the desirable figure that others are mesmerized by. This Narcissist Power can be used by anyone: Others see and believe us to be what we see and believe ourselves to be. I have tested this age-old belief and have projected exaggerated smiles and brightness when out-and-about even though I felt like doing otherwise, and as a result, I have gathered an enamored following. Try it yourself.

Narcissists are extremely judgmental and fixated on the appearance of others. My Sociopath repeatedly told me that he had a photographic memory when it comes to people and the first time that he saw me over at Turk Narc's house, he remembered how I wore my hair and the color of my clothing. Turk Narc and My Sociopath knew each other through the clannish Turkish community in the San Diego area. Narcissists believe themselves to be aesthetes or experts in beauty.

Of course, when My Sociopath and I became intimate fifteen years later, as a result of my rebounding from Turk Narc, I was the best looking, most perfect-in-height/weight, skin, hair color, hand-shape and overall form on this planet; these Narcissist declarations went as far back as his first seeing me all those years ago. When a Narcissist has control over a target or enabler, and she is feeding his ego, he sees her as perfection because he believes his own perfected look is worthy of the same. Any woman wants to believe she is the most beautiful and desirable so this fed my low self-esteem. Because I am an Empath, I too thought My Sociopath was the handsomest man ever. In actuality, he is far from good looking. The honeymoon period puts us in a trance and we are also delusional.

Empaths love deeply and we don't notice the looks of people and when we are smitten, we love the looks of the person we deeply care about. But wait, Narcissists really love the looks of the targets they are enthralled with! The difference is, Empaths love a person's physical appearance because we see their soul represented on the outside. A Narcissist sees a new target's image as ideal because he believes she will be The All Mothering Spirit plus Sex Goddess that will take away his emptiness. He glorifies his mother's looks and so too will he yours...until...His ideal beauty waivers according to the person who is filling his ego needs to the deepest and most nurturing level.

However, our extreme "gorgeousness" quickly fades in the eyes of a Narcissist when the honeymoon period ends and real life starts, and once we start showing concern over and questioning his lies, half-truths, distortions and his sabotaging acts in our environment: We become fat, ugly and too old. Soon, every other possible source of Socio/Narc Supply will become "beautiful" and we will witness his numb look when anyone of a sexual nature comes near him. He is a sex-addict and is fantasizing about a new Mother and Sex Love that will complete him. You will be driven nuts and feel as if you are insane with jealousy. The Devalue stage destroys our sense-of-self; we absorb and believe in his projected devalue.

When I told My Sociopath that I could no longer tolerate the madness and my adoring eyes turned away from ever loving him again, he hissed hateful words at me: "Your neck and chest are wrinkling." He is 13 years older than me, overweight and balding and he is not considered a handsome man. I am what people would consider a natural and classic beauty but have never felt good about myself and as a result, downplay my looks (a perfect target for a socio/narc). Sociopaths are masters at switching reality. However, I decided to make his cruel words work in my favor by finally taking care of my looks and thus propelling myself toward health and vitality. We age dramatically when with a Narcissist. Stress really does kill.

Side Note: Narcissists see themselves as the strongest and best of all humans but yet they are hypochondriacs. They manifest hypochondria when they are not getting the intense attention they crave; they become "sick" from the point of their inner-disconnect. It is a "cry" for ego-filling or for someone to show them care and concern so that they can feel momentarily grounded. Non-disordered people have a spiritual cord that connects the soul with the mind, and to the brain, and to the heart to manifest personality or our solid beliefs, morals, drives, attitudes, characteristics and behaviors expressed out into the world. Narcissists are not connected to a spiritual cord. Every time I caught My Sociopath in a lie and was leaving him, he became "sick" or "injured." This is a Narcissist's cry out to the universe that he is lost and "falling" into his inner abyss of nothingness; he is detached from humanness and floating away.

I've spent most of my life in relationships with older men and the various people we've encountered as we were out-and-about as a couple tend to make the same typical and unthinking comments that we make a "great-looking" couple. These comments mostly come from unthinking men that also have warped egos and instead of finding "an old, ugly man – beautiful, younger woman" couple inappropriate, they glorify The Narcissist and believe he is with his perfect match. But more importantly, The Narcissist himself has no ability to see the inappropriateness of our match-up as he believes himself to be the same age and quality and that he is the one exuding the beauty. In situations such as this, I stand idly by with a confused half-smile and allow the Narcissist to stand in the showering compliments of him being the younger and more beautiful half-of-our-pair. I feel old and out-of-place around people younger than myself; Narcissists rarely get this feeling.

The Narcissist will no doubt call you names and insult your physical appearance when you catch him at his games but the insults will be at their most during the Final Discard. I am a thinly built woman, which was always "admired" by My Sociopath and he despised what he referred to as the "short, round, plump" build of a typical Turkish woman. Why did he loathe this look so much? Because his other ex-wife was Turkish, had this look, and she hated him for his destruction. I was the opposite and considered perfection...actually, I was only Honeymoon Perfection because he was getting sex, money, free work and care-taking services out of me without attached responsibility. On a break during our divorce proceedings, My Sociopath yelled down the hallway at me: *You have a skinny ass and my new 27 year old wife has a huge, round ass.* My Sociopath remarried another Turkish woman before our divorce was final. Sociopaths are walking, talking, breathing contradictions.

Not only was this a six year old having a tantrum against his former recess friend, but My Sociopath's proof-cry that when it comes to another one of his badly ending relationships, he was the right one, the superior one, and all because he immediately flew into a new "love" relationship. Another relationship jump, without discerning quality of match in the partner, as proof that he is the "good, loved, desired" and hence, I am the "bad, unloved, undesired."

Narcissists never take breaks between relationships to grow, to evolve, or to become independent entities. He will even mock you as he exposes you to his new target and his crowd of enablers that you are *still alone*. This is his proof that you are *The Lone Defect* and he merely tolerated you until it was inevitable that he had to break it off with you. Normal people don't relationship jump but take individual time for reflection and growth and would be embarrassed to jump right into another relationship immediately after the ending of a so-called abusive one.

It has been more than two years since divorcing My Sociopath, more than three years since separation, and his aging process has been cruel. He now stands as a 60 year old pregnant looking woman with testosterone draining out of him - forming puddles at his feet - next to a 30 year old Turkish woman. He proudly displays his desperate torment all over the internet. This is his disorder manifested for all to see: A picture that desperately tries to present a flash in time, a distortion of reality, that he continues to be *loved.* Just a short time later, this young Turkish woman looks old and sickly, just as I did when with My Sociopath. He is displaying himself as if he is a powerful Sultan in charge of a Harem of beautiful and well-taken care of concubines. Narcissists have no concept of reality though its dreadful existence is apparent in pictures. They just had a baby together and they are miserable...how sad...for the baby.

I am healing, good days mixed with more challenging ones...this is real beauty and in the long run, it will endure.

The Aging Narcissist

I find older men attractive because I think they are more settled, reliable, mature, dependable, and full of wisdom because of living through and experiencing many life lessons. I am an Old Soul and I have a hard time relating to people my age. However, these positive attributes have not been the case with the older men that I've met. **Older men (and women) that compulsively search for and go through strings of love and sexual relationships but never achieve long-term success are dangerous.** Men who were even slightly narcissistic when younger become more Narcissistic Desperate as they grow older: They emotionally go into a panic because their sexual prowess is decreasing and their pool of new ego-supply is lessening.

When the Narcissist was 35-years-old, even a half-decent looking 35 year old, he could charm and manipulate anyone 20 to 60-years-old (approximately). That's a pool of targets that span 40 years! When he is 60, he can maybe, on his luckiest day, nab a 45 year old, but he will have to work harder because not only will the 45 year old be looking at the 28 year olds, but she's not as dumb as she once was. Narcissists don't put a lot of effort into anything. (My Sociopath was able to capture a significantly younger target but she was desperate to get to the US and he portrayed himself as a rich, American business man. There are situations out of the norm but usually the sociopath is wealthy - young women don't want poor, old men.)

When Narcissists were young, attention and glamour came easily, naturally and without effort. They must cling to their youth to preserve their quick and easy access to attention sources. This is why Narcissists try to look and portray themselves younger than they are: hair color, plastic surgery, youthful clothing, excessive working out of the body (when the face falls, pump up the body) and surrounding themselves with younger people.

The 60 year old Narcissist can perhaps swoon a 68 year old but she may not fall as hard for him and be as glowingly receptive toward his charm. Even then, at its best, this pool of ego-sources from when he was 35 has been cut-in-half to 23 years...from maybe getting a 45 year old to maybe a 68 year old. Plus, ego-supply sources in these age groups have more cemented-in lives and habits and they are less willing to succumb to Narcissist control. A woman in her 60s may have property and assets from a previous husband and family so she will not so quickly bring a new man into her home. Women in these age-ranges are more likely to veer away from men that show red flags.

A Narcissist is worn out by his 50s because of the sheer number of relationships that he's gone through, and not to mention the years of highs and lows involved in all these relationships. An extreme Narc/Socio has a bunch of ex-wives and many children by different women. He is financially, emotionally and physically exhausted in his later years trying to keep up with the demands of all his different children that range in ages through decades. Narcissists/Sociopaths start having children at 20 and inappropriately have them in their 40s, 50s and 60s; they are taking care of young children most of their lives. They put all their energy into being the favorite parent, not the best parent, and turn their adult children into "Surrogate Partners." These adult children (with the help of their mothers) manipulate this and use the Narc's need for attention for their advantage.

He is very susceptible to being taken advantage of as he gets older because his love-bombing sources dry up and he depends more upon secondary ego-sources (adult children, family, acquaintances, "friends"). In order to keep people around him at all times, he knows that he needs to be a favor-doer and generous entertainer; everyone is using the aging Narc Dad, Narc Ex and Narc "Friend."

A Narcissist turns resentful as he ages because his young and energetic days of commanding all the attention and having instant access to willing victims that fall easily under his influence withers away. His sexual prowess days are declining and he realizes his sexual energy is no longer his leading force. He no longer has all the bright and shining faces smiling upon him. If anything, people are only using him. He realizes his looks and overall attraction are fading and he will start experiencing bouts of depression and anxiety. Therefore, his last-ditch efforts for new ego sources become more intensified.

As we get older, we become more desperate for love and therefore, more vulnerable to the hoards of Narcissistic men who are clamoring around out there desperately seeking sexual objects. Older men who had mild sexual addictions when younger become more sexually obsessed as they get older. They are in mad pursuit to regain the time in their life when women moaned and groaned under their *manly hardness.* They must seek more intense and abundant experiences, with just about anyone, to get that same sexual feel or energy they experienced decades ago. This is where an older woman is vulnerable to the charming advances of what appears to be an older man that wants to settle down with a good woman to lead a good life when in fact, this man is a megalomaniac and opportunist that is primarily seeking pleasure, care-taking and ego-strokes.

Aging is not just a process of growing older but of developing wisdom upon a foundation of knowledge. It is the expansion of consciousness through the interweaving, blending and uniting of the subjective essence of quality. It is seeing through nonsense and distinguishing between what is important and what is superficial and ego gratification.

Misery comes to those whose life-time focus was on unreal, external validation and the means to real, internal validation was never developed. There is no growth or stability in the external; only our internal selves can be steady in its movement toward knowing quality and truth. Narcissists are not capable of internal validation, hence, their mad pursuit of chasing people-sources for redemption. This is the lifetime battle they fight against the misery of never finding harmony and quality within.

THREE

THEIR MOTHERS

She Bore Eggs

My Sociopath was always ravished but had dead taste buds. I am convinced that all sensory organs are deadened in sociopaths making them need a constant and high-level of external stimulation in all areas of life: people attention; new targets with fresh, exciting sex; flirtation; hypochondria with doctors, emergency room visits, and medications; the creation of drama between members of his social surroundings; and visual stimulation (images on facebook and porn addictions).

My Sociopath only cared about food in so far that a past, current or future target prepared it for him. This brought him back into Mother's Womb for a moment in time. He connects a woman's food preparation with Mothering Essence of deep nourishment (literal and spiritual). He was always starving and devouring food. I spent hours making dishes and grand Turkish dinners from scratch; I was the ultimate Mothering Spirit but in the end, this was not enough. A Sociopath is never satiated.

This is also linked to a Sociopath's high energy level and the fact that they are always on the prowl. Think about a lion in the jungle: Hungry and in need of food to satiate starvation. Sociopaths are spiritually starved and need to constantly fill their emptiness. Though I was diligently feeding all his needs (literally and figuratively), he fell in love with a woman who brought deviled-eggs to a potluck. He obsessively and embarrassingly followed The

Deviled-Egg Woman around and for months repeated to me, not only of her Greatness In Deviled-Egg Creation (she too was embarrassed by this attention to her eggs and exclaimed, *I only added mustard and mayonnaise*), but of her entire Out-of-World-Mothering-Essence and the inferiority of the man she was engaged to. He knew nothing about either of these two individuals; he only knew she bore eggs.

I notice a link from manipulating, lying, and controlling people going back to their mothers. The mothers are one of the following:

1. Emotionally cold and detached.

2. Over-indulging, enabling and obsessively attached to her children and/or gene pool.

3. Cycles through both extremes (unstable or bipolar).

The following tendencies and/or disorders in their children come to mind. I include Empaths because they repeatedly allow themselves to be destroyed; this is not a healthy sense-of-self. Narcissists seem to emerge from all three types of mothers. Of course, there are always exceptions and there are people that turn out well-adjusted and enlightened despite their mothers.

1. Cold, emotionally detached mother = Child of all extremes from Empath to Narcissist to Sociopath and even to Autistic and Asperger's

2. Over-indulging, enabling mother = Child that is Primarily Narcissistic

3. Unstable mother that cycles through emotional extremes of giving and taking away love = Child that is Primarily Borderline with traits of narcissism, empathy and people-pleasing

The cold and emotionally detached mother may have suffered the same abuse and/or neglect as a child. This is the mother that creates children of all extremes from the Sociopath to the Empath and perhaps to Autistic/Asperger's. This is my mother. My grandmother died when my mother was 12 years old whereby leaving my mother in the care of her older siblings. My grandfather was there but not involved. Even before my grandmother died, she did not give my mother the love, teachings, guidance and compassion that a girl needs from her mother. Finally, to have a parent die at the time of puberty dramatically affects healthy emotional development. It is sometimes the case that people without a loving and compassionate childhood role-model are not able to provide this to their own children. As a result, my mother could never emotionally attach to her children. However, emotionally cold mothers can also produce the flip version, an Empath, or a person that gives to the world what he/she craves to receive.

I taught students with autism and Asperger's syndrome for many years and I observed that the mothers (and many fathers) were similar to one another. The mothers were highly-intelligent, yet constricted in their emotions, very cold and stern in appearance and little expenditure of an outward appearance of genuine love and warmth. They came across very detached and removed from natural and innate loving; they seemed disconnected, confined, and without an expanding nature. However, they were intensely focused on their child as far as being strict and procedural advocates in institutions such as the schools and other health and mental care systems. I have no doubt they loved their child, but their love didn't radiate a carefree warmth.

When I was in the presence of these parents, it was as if I were up against rigidness. These mothers (and some fathers) seem to have mild Asperger's themselves. I believe my mother has a mild form of Asperger's or even autism (explained later). Can there be this mother-link between the brain development of those who grow up to have a personality disorder and those who develop Autism Spectrum Disorder? I'm in no way saying these are the same disorders because Empaths can destroy themselves, Narcissists destroy other people and those with autism and Asperger's syndrome do not destroy. However, I am saying that perhaps the disorders are linked to not receiving a balance of carefree love and warmth with gentle but effective boundaries. I use "mother" as the main example, and "father" as secondary because our emotional condition is formed more by the mother.

The over-indulging and enabling mother who creates primarily Narcissists, throws love without boundaries at her children but she does not have emotional love that is expressed outward toward humanity. She is conventional, narrow-minded and constricted in her love toward others but excessive in doting on her children; it is entitlement. If you are confused why "conventional" can be a negative trait, think of it this way: A Christian who believes he is living a conventional and righteous life shouts to his neighbor that he "has to be a Christian and saved in order to gain entry into heaven." This is not acting with pure love toward one's fellow man but instead harshly ostracizing someone else for not being, believing or behaving like oneself. Indeed, this non-Christian neighbor may do more good for humanity than the condemning Christian.

The over-indulging mother creates a sense of self-entitlement in her child.

The Narcissist's mother feels that in not teaching boundaries, discipline or empathy that she is providing unconditional love or is displaying the ultimate expression of a loving mother. This mother is not intelligently aware of her child's tendency toward apathy unless taught kindness toward all. The mother feels her son is superior because he is an output of herself or he is Her Genetics; he is her carbon copy. Blind devotion to anything, including family, overrides intelligent discernment and judgement. She brainwashes her son - long into his old-age years - that he only has "trouble" with women because these women are "bad" and he only deserves the most magnificent woman or more specifically, someone just like her! Basically, he must find an over-indulging lover that feeds his sense of entitlement, aka, his Narcissism.

The over-indulging mother stands by and watches the repetitive and destructive habits of her son and accepts it as his greatness and of his partner's inferiority; this mother lacks authentic compassion and empathy for others outside her genetic gene pool.

Narcissists are women haters and they are a strong force behind female oppression and abuse in societies all over the world. An over-indulging and enabling mother can contribute to this force with her lack of empathy toward women she considers lower standing or inferior. This mother is into superficial image, the shallow significance of family names, and what a woman can offer her son as far as prestige and security. Therefore, a hardworking woman that provides for and supports herself through hard times, without strong family support, is deemed unworthy. In actuality, this hardworking and self-sufficient woman proves herself to be more worthy than a woman that relies upon a family name and is dependent upon family support and money. In current times, many women, however hardworking and with pure and honest souls, fall into this *lower and weaker class* of lacking family strength and support that this mother frowns upon. Finally, the most harmful result of an enabling mother, is when she stands quietly by as her son leaves a woman depleted and destitute. Older women must protect younger women no matter what her son enacts on his intimate partner and despite the excuses he gives for doing so.

Children require unconditional love and nurturing without the essence of rigidness and mental control and without emotional overindulgence. This unconditional love must not only be given with emotional warmth and openness (not genetic based) but with boundaries that include discipline, guidance and the teachings of kindness and love toward all.

The atmosphere of love is not an emotional, sentimental form of love but is based upon a realization of the potentialities of the child as an Individual, with a sense of true Responsibility. Most children's natures are warped by the rush and hurry of those with whom they are perforce associated. An atmosphere of order is needed wherein the child can learn responsibility (Bailey, Education In The New Age, 76).

Unstable, Bipolar or Borderline mothers that create a primarily Borderline child with traits of narcissism, empathy and/or people-pleasing tendencies, have drastic fluctuations in their moods and this results in her

<u>constant giving and taking away of her love and attention</u>. This entails periods of detachment or withdrawing into her own psychological illness mixed with periods of pulling her child strongly into her, without boundaries, to fulfill her selfish needs for devoted attention and love. The child is on this roller-coaster ride of getting shunned aside (feeling discarded) and then receiving intense love without boundaries (feeling self-entitled), and he is not only confused, but needs the drug-high of the intense love period. He becomes fixated and addicted to his mother's wild expressions of love episodes and becomes her caretaker during her detached periods. Her love is exhilarating and intoxicating. An unstable mother does not enforce healthy boundaries, nor is she a strong leader and teacher for her child; the child must serve her needs instead; he is either her entertainer or her burden. These mothers create tantrum-throwing adults that grab desperately at love and then have a fit when they perceive the slightest nip to ego.

The child of an unstable mother will do anything to win over the love given sporadically from his elusive mother. He is a people-pleaser. Later in life, he may seek out Apath women that withhold sex and love. He will fight to win her love and people-please her more all the while neglecting the truly kind and loving woman that is devoted to him because she is too easy (the empath). The loving and stable woman that gives him consistent love is not a challenge, is not out of reach like his mother, does not torment his soul and ego and therefore, he will abuse her, drain her of her love, and all the while devoting his real love (his version of "love") to the detached and withholding source.

All these mothers are not emotionally or mentally measured or consistent. Just like his mother loved with conditions, so he will too.

A horrific car accident killed Turk Narc's father and though his mother was a passenger of his death ride, she didn't cry or have an emotional reaction. Turk Narc turned this into one of his mother's many saintly attributes and that she was "strong" and "brave" and was "saving her children from grief." This mother failed to role model for her son a healthy expression of emotions connected to love and loss.

Turk Narc's mother is over-indulging and thought no woman was ever good enough for her son. An emotionally healthy mother would NOT create a man with thoughts of his superiority to women and would instead send him out into the world with an instilled sense of goodwill toward all, especially women.

Mr.Oh has four failed marriages and produced six children by three different women; he too talks of his "Perfect and Saintly Mother." He later revealed to me that she was bipolar and retreated for months at a time into the darkness of her bedroom and when she came out, she was the grandest, most beautiful and fascinating woman ever; they would stay up all night together during her manic episodes doing exhilarating activities and being *best friends.*

Many Socios/Narcs/Borderlines call their mothers by their first names and refer to them as their "best friends."

My Sociopath honored his mother but had intermittent flashes of trauma memory in connection to her. He filled with bitterness and hate regarding her periods of emotional vacancy and mostly, her neglect in protecting him against the father and pampering this man instead of him.

The emotional processing differences between extreme and blind Mother Worship without seeing her weaknesses, and that of conflicted feelings of hate and trauma flashes, may determine the fine line between narcissism and sociopathy.

Their mothers created an emotional body within them that craves constant mother-love stimulation stemming from either too much indulgence, or not enough love...overall lack of healthy moderation and boundaries. His brain is miswired to see women as sources for devoted mother love and this results in the frantic honeymoon period to gain unconditional love and acceptance from a new source (one that he hasn't ruined). He is seeking Mother's Womb, literally, through sex, and figuratively, through her nurturing essence. This dramatic period always ends because that teenage love feeling between intimate partners fades from honeymoon lust to conditional love based on responsibility, dependability, trustworthiness and loyalty. Narcissists cannot handle anything with responsibility and conditions; he wants to live forever as a little boy smothered by the love of his mother.

He is in the constant search for Romantic Sex Goddess Lust mixed with Mother Essence Unconditional Love.

A Narcissist does not even realize he is a destroyer; he truly believes he is The Victim...The Victim of a bad woman that did not provide him with all encompassing and consuming love like a mother. He constantly perceives slights and disrespects from her because she is supposed to hold and coddle him to her breast despite his big, bad-man behaviors. The Narcissist is a woman-hater because no woman can ever give him full love and acceptance without expectations for his proper behavior.

Accurately Seeing Mother

We don't really wake up until our 40s or later. I never connected the dots until recently...the dots that my mother was just as sick as my father: She was no victim to him; she participated in destroying her children. Barbara Hand Clow states that we wake up emotionally between 42-44 and have another awakening at 51 (YouTube). I believe this 42-44 is more around 49. Our 20s and 30s are spent trying to become educated, traveling, looking for love or a soul mate, creating and struggling in careers, and trying to make our own home and family. For those who suffered from childhood abuse or neglect, these years are spent in not only doing these things, but in fighting for our lives through bad education and career choices, bad partner choosing and unhealthy habits. We are either struggling to survive or looking ahead, not back. Therefore, we do not accurately process our childhood circumstances and see our parents in a clear light until later in life.

Men are even less likely to do this accurate reflection of their parents, especially their mothers. Men tend to glamorize their mothers, especially enabling, overly doting and indulging, non-disciplinarian and non-boundary setting mothers: the "best friend" mothers. The other end of the spectrum are men who deny that they are negatively affected by the abuse of a cold, neglecting, and unloving mother. Because most women are more emotional, they have an easier time accessing these realizations than do men. This is why the daughters from these homes are often outcasted and gaslighted with contradictory words from others that "everything was fine," while her brothers seem to sincerely believe there were no real problems.

It takes a long time, most of our adult lives, if ever, to see that our 'victim-parent' may have been just as abusive as the other parent. We don't usually see this because the loud, tantrum throwing, physically threatening parent overshadows the behaviors of the more emotionally abusive parent. As I entered my 40s, I saw something in my mind: Where was my mother when HE was severely beating us and locking us in the dark basement for hours? Why did she never sneak into our rooms to tell us it would be okay? Why did she choose to work all the time when she didn't need to for financial reasons and no other mother in our 1980's neighborhood was working...therefore, leaving us alone for 10-hours at a time with him? Why, when the rare chance she was our caretaker, and he was at work, and we did something that upset her (normal child things like arguing with one another or rough playing), she called him at work in hysterics insisting he come home? She **sicked** him on us. Why did HE come to me when I was 14 to tell me that I wasn't supposed to wear a bra to bed at night? Where was SHE?

Just a short time ago, my mother hissed at me through the phone: *What about me! I was afraid to come home to find you dead and blood everywhere.* My poor mother...finding me murdered by my father would have been awful.

Children have a protective shield in their brain for survival that keeps them lovingly devoted to their mother and sometimes this blindness is forever. My mother couldn't deal with her children's emotions or their humanness; we were mechanical or physical objects only (even our physical unnerved her)...she worked to get away from him, from us, and thus my brothers and I were laid at his mercy. We cannot fathom, as members of the human species, that our mothers are not made of pure and perfect love. Some people never wake up to the true nature of their mother, or parents, or childhood home. For those of us who do wake up and look back to see things that we never saw before, we can use this awakening for growth.

I had to start waking up: It was if there was a radar device in my heart...I fell into relationships with closed-off men and was driven to crack them wide open to love me when they were incapable of love. After all, I was the greatest love-source available to a disturbed man: I was my mother, a sacrificer of hearts. However, I only ever sacrificed my own heart.

FOUR

THE GANG

Female Supporters

We fool ourselves into believing that because we are in the 2010s, there is no longer sexism and women are just as equal as men. This is not the case. Women can vote, obtain higher educational degrees, are employees, supervisors and CEOs in the workforce. They are single mothers, heads of households and can get tattoos and piercings. However, all this does not mean female equality in the soul consciousness of humanity. Humans operate instinctively and women are more innately caretakers, nurturers, empaths, tolerant, accepting, and patient. Men are more emotionally removed and mentally controlled; they are more capable of tending to life-survival matters and can more powerfully manage and defend their environment.

When a Narcissist "cries" about his victimization by his intimate partner to a female supporter, she will immediately go into save mode. This is female instinct. There is something beyond sad and pathetic about a grown man, seemingly powerful, broken down and crying over how horrible his woman is treating him. It is like the toddler boy weeping to himself on a playground and all the little girls and mothers flock to his rescue. Compare this to our gut instinct when a little girl is crying on a playground. Sure, others will congregate to see what is happening, but it is not as heartrending as the little weeping boy. I cried all the time as a little girl at the hands of my abusive father and vacant mother, but there was nothing more horrific for me than to see my brothers cry, who in so many ways represented little crying men. We expect women to cry because they are emotional and sensitive. Men are the strong, stoic, and powerful and when they are in tears (even crocodile tears) it defies the natural state of nature and fervently triggers a woman's mothering and protection instincts.

The female victim of a Narcissist takes on the appearance of an out-of-control wreck. She is not so sympathetic in appearance and can be the target of attack by not only The Narcissist's female supporters but by males as well. There are some males that will swoop into aid a woman crying of her victimization but it does not evolve in the same way as does the female primitive instinct to protect the shattered male. In many cases, the male-*saver* wants to have sex with the crying victim to make her "feel better."

The male narcissist can have many women in his support group because they motherly protect him from the horrible woman that he is entwined with by consoling him during and after her awfulness. In return, he is somehow aiding these women in fatherly, husbandly or handyman ways. My Sociopath offers women repair work and handyman favors. What woman doesn't need her own personal handyman? Most of My Sociopath's female supporters and enablers are divorced with and without children, or simply shattered women that need a "man" figure in their life to feel "protected." The feeling of protection is reciprocal between the male narcissist and female supporter. However, My Sociopath hurries through repairs, does poor quality work, or claims that it is beyond fixable when he realizes the repair may take too much time or effort. The female supporter feels that he, at the least, tried, and gladly accepts whatever low-quality or lack of effort he throws at her; she anticipates that he will be there in the future if needed. My Sociopath now seems to have completed his obligation for the female supporter and she remains in his corner for when he needs to access her pity and support against another one of his victims.

THE GANG

There are a lot of women roaming around out there that will use a man, though he has a partner, for his handyman favors or to simply get out for the evening on his tab. We are at an unprecedented time in history where we have hoards of women that are single or divorced and many have children that still demand their attention. Many of these women are under or uneducated with low-level skills and are fighting to survive on their own in this horrible economy that lacks decent jobs, security and benefits. It is often the case that these women are using men that have partners in distress at home. The enabling "female friend" and Narcissist *feed* one another.

My parents never lived in this type of world with these dynamics. My father took care of his home (though he was extremely abusive, he was still there) and other men took care of their homes. The world was not filled with this needy-woman energy lurking everywhere that Narcissists use for supporters and enablers when they are in the midst of destroying their intimate partner and family. It was unheard of, not long ago, for a single woman to interfere in the life of a married or attached man; now, it is common practice. These women allow narcissistic men to thrive and to better destroy their families because he feels he has a herd of waiting and adoring women out there; these supporting females are fueling his *I'm a Victim* Story and his narcissism to leave his partner instead of staying to work things out. He is supported in not being loyal, true, steadfast and committed to those at home. Facebook makes this play even easier. Everyone is lurking around on social media fantasizing that every other person is amazing besides their partner. So many people, especially Narcissists, are smitten by mere image alone and live in fantasy-land of all the better options waiting in the queue.

The female supporters that play this game with dangerous males have no sense of self-worth and are not guided by a grounded and solid belief system or clear set of thought processes and boundaries of proper behavior. They are man-less and will take any man that wants to do them favors. They make up a large percentage of the non-thinkers in our world or those who do nothing beyond going with the flow; many of these women are Apaths. They are easily manipulated and swayed into staying in the social circle of a man that they unthinkingly believe is a helper and male protector in their lonely lives; they are desperate for social connections and a sense-of-protection that a male offers. These type of women will always stand by the male narcissist and make him stronger each time he goes through chaos and destruction with another target; they have nothing to lose but will now and then get some help in their lives. When he is in turmoil with his intimate partner, the female enabler can squeeze herself into the crevices of another one of his shattering relationships to get more favors done.

This herd of female supporters make it easy for The Narcissist to perpetuate his illusion that he is a good and safe man. The new target comes along and thinks because he has so many *solid*, female "friends" that he is an honorable man and overall respected in his community. Combine this with his tales of abuse and neglect by his partner at home (or ex) and that so many "female friends" adore him, you have a new target that is fooled into believing he is a man of superior quality. The new target falls into a sense of security in thinking since he has such strong female allies, he is good toward all women.

The female supporter solidifies her herd member status by promoting The Narcissist's victimization stories to the new target while simultaneously pumping up new target's ego that she is so much better than the previous target. This keeps female supporter on the good side of both The Narcissist and the new target and thus in The Narcissist Herd. We feel honored to be his One True Love and believe in our amazing woman qualities that we are able to make Great Man happy and be placed as The Primary Love in Great Man's Herd. In actuality, the previously discarded herd member (now ex or soon ex) probably got fed up with a female enabler lurking around in the shadows, emotionally supporting The Narcissist in his abuse toward her and providing him a safety-net for his insanity, and as a result, confronted her on her inappropriate behaviors. This created more of the teaming up between The Narcissist and female enabler against the current target.

The female supporter/enabler was part of his entourage that took down the previous ex's social-surroundings via gossip, spreading of lies and half-truths, and the ganging up attacks: She was Herd Member Smear-Campaign Worker. This female supporter/enabler will always end up back-stabbing the newest target in favor of maintaining her Narcissist Herd Membership. You will notice that the female supporters of Narcissists do not have solid male partners, female friendships or family relations. They likely have a mental or personality disorder as well.

When The Narcissist first acquires his new target, he no longer needs the female supporter and will shove her to a back-shelf until the chaos of his new relationship starts. He will then pull her off the shelf to back him up during the chaos.

The strongest female supporter My Sociopath has is an older, heavy-set, real estate agent. Once My Sociopath won me over, he had no use for her and he ran and hid when she visited our business. His excuse was that she was "fat and unattractive" and "didn't look like this when they first met." Sociopaths are shallow and have no real loyalty toward anyone. I was in shock that he thought of his great "female friend" this way and I went into protection mode to help save her feelings from the Hiding Sociopath in the back room of our business. I was not only trying to protect another female, I was trying to protect what he told me was their "great friendship." I spent hours nicely talking to her and was delayed in getting important work done as My Sociopath hid out in a dark, dank, back room trolling facebook for other "female friends." Not even the most loyal "female friends" are safe from his disloyalty.

Now and then Real Estate Lady caught My Sociopath at our business before he managed to hide. He immediately went into a housing and property dialog with her promising that she would be involved in all our future real estate transactions. Narcissists are always expecting supporters/enablers to give them something for nothing. He was hoping she had secret real estate knowledge on something that could be purchased at a bargain. During this time, he promised our property transactions to four other real estate agents who visited our business. Many days we never had real customers but only long trails of people in and out who were expecting repair favors and My Sociopath expecting special treatment from them. When we finally made a small real estate transaction, My Sociopath used a fifth agent that we didn't even know, and who walked into our business immediately prior to the purchase. Narcissists not only lack loyalty but they choose the most current adoring source that is standing in front of them; they have no focus or long-term memory and are extremely disorganized. When Real Estate Lady, long time supporter, found this out, he blamed me for not liking her and it was my choice to go with the other agent. She believed him. People not using their brains for discernment: I was nothing but gracious toward her and The Hiding Sociopath was nothing but a Fair Weather Friend.

There is no real joy circulating in The Sociopath Circle; only strained feelings between everyone.

Female supporters of Narcissists are not protectors of other women, cannot find their own intimate partners, and just want an essence of maleness around their lives and will turn blindly and dumbly away from the path of destruction he seems to live on. Women are instinctively driven to seek male attention believing in their protection when often times, this is not the case. Males are innately stronger and feel themselves to be protectors of women, but some are destroyers.

He will have sex with a female supporter when he is desperate or having a hard time pinning down the next target. However, he will use her for a transitional source of stimulation and dump her as soon as someone *better* comes along. It is his choice whether she will be his intimate partner and he can take his time at this decision because he knows that she will always be lingering around in the background. She, however, lives in quiet desperation that someday, between various other "horrible" women, he will choose her. But mostly, there is something about the female enabler that deterred him from being with her intimately to begin with. Again, Narcissists are very shallow and though she had been endlessly loyal and devoted to him, it could be something as insignificant as her weight, teeth, or breath!

Females must start protecting one another...men protect each other!

Support Team

Narcissists have no inner compass for a good or bad human. Attention and stimulation is all they seek from those around them. Most do not care about the quality of the human; it is the quantity of attention and stimulation that they receive that matters. Narcissists are constantly surrounded by a group of supporters and they must be the center of attention. Some of these supporters are consistent and there is also a rotating flock; a circulating flow of newly won over people with those that fade away. He gains followers by honing in on weakness and/or portraying himself as a big-brother or 'leader of the team.' In turn, the weak-minded feel privileged that they associate with such a *powerful* person.

Narcissists spend their lives going from one distracting human-object to the next.

A supporter or enabler of anyone, especially of a Narcissist, is someone who operates primarily on an emotional level and they do not use their intelligence. When many of these people come together to form a herd there is a group attraction or magnetic pull to The Narcissist and it is a rare person that can engage their brain and step away from this group. Narcissists create a characteristic, or tendency of the group, and will avoid people who do not fall under this hypnotizing spell of devotion toward him.

Turk Narc kept the magnetic pull of his support group strong by being the wild, out-of-control, party boy (though he was too old for this) that was all about fun times; he was the life or energy of every gathering. He kept a support group of people who, like himself, did nothing important in their lives and had no other priorities but to party, to be selfish and to seek instant gratification. I was the serious, more intelligent thinking and acting, the one who worked for greater creations on this earth (I was doing animal rescue work, getting an MA., teaching and advocating for special education students), so when there were violations against me by Turk Narc, I was turned into the sensitive one of the group and was pushed to the fringes as an outcast. I wasn't a non-thinking, shallow, party girl, but serious and discerning in quality. Narcissists take intimate partner issues to The Herd so that she will be slaughtered. **This is a sure sign of the personality disordered: healthy people deal with issues in privacy and never incite gang mentality.**

My Sociopath lives by: "I'll do this for you, you do this for me." Sociopaths target the most needy in society for their support team and even those individuals have something of worth to offer. My Sociopath has a group of refugees from Afghanistan and Iraq that he helps with their paperwork and US bureaucratic matters and they do extreme favors for him in return. He pays them $10.00/day for working at his business and for acting as false witnesses and supporters in all his problems...but in addition to their government refugee payment and benefits, this money is significant. Plus, Iraqis and Afghans get to hang out in the US with a Great Ottoman Turk.

The blind supporters stay emotionally connected and in a magnetic hold to The Narcissist because they find their security in his emotional steadiness (it's actually his emotional disconnect), high energy and in his favor doing and promises. The current target is the nice one that is being whittled away raw and exuding a heightened state of frazzled emotions and therefore, she is the moving target...she is not a permanent source in The Narcissist's life and the supporters know this because of his constant complaining about her...even before she is devalued and discarded, she is considered insignificant.

An Open Person, An Empath

Open people search most of their lives for true friends and many of us struggle to find this. We are constantly searching for a soul connection of loyalty, honesty, genuineness and authenticity. We long to make connections with others who are working to build positive creations on this earth and especially those who are working for similar causes as we are. Since we have a strong connection to all humanity, and we especially connect with the energy of the earth and all its animals, we search for these traits in everyone we meet, and despite not catching sight of any, we instead visualize with our heart a light in the dark cavernous corners of even the most destructive beings. We reflect ourselves onto everything and into everyone, and see goodness in all...even though it is not there.

A Narcissist seeks an Empath for his closest and most intimate partner because she will give the most without receiving much in return. She is kind, honest and loyal to a fault, often self-deprecating, operates mostly heart center, and is a natural healer. She will be found in non-glorified and unappreciated professions that exhaust her life-energy such as special education, nursing, social work, and counseling. She has strong intuition but will push these traits away to fit in with society and especially the predators that she attracts.

The Empath's good and loving nature combined with the renewed energy he gains from the support group because he is with someone new excites him; he presents an image of their great love and she radiates light into his Dark Herd. The Narcissist appears lively and filled with positive energy when he is with the Empath. The Empath feels like an accepted member of his herd until there is a relationship issue and it requires his dedication, steadfastness and commitment. He then dramatically turns on her, makes her an enemy of not only himself, but the social group, and he is now stimulated by the drama of her being "crazy." She immediately goes from being a light in his life and in the group to being the enemy of the group. Hence, he has pulled his support group closer together in their fight against a common enemy and he is re-energized by his victim status.

The Narcissist is a walking corpse and only has a superficial vibration that is temporarily activated by his "Fresh" source of love and attention. This is not his soul's vibration for he does not have his own center of fiery energy...he lacks an internal Sphere of Fire. What seems like his high vibration is a resonance from the shallow and meaningless displays in his environment.

In an intimate relationship, Empaths will continually forgive the unforgivable, give repeated chances, doubt perceptions of the treatment, feel bad when The Narcissist does something horrible and we have a normal reaction, put ourselves on a lower level than The Narcissist despite our many accomplishments, and overlook the disparity between our good and purposeful driven life and his low-quality existence. We see ourselves as equals, even to the most discarded in society. The Narcissist can control us and we allow it because we are operating heart and we are seeing his soul despite its harmful patterns. On a higher level of consciousness (without our knowledge), we are trying to pull The Narcissist along, out of his darkness and into our light. All along, we do not understand that The Narcissist is bringing us down into his hell.

Open people are also very receptive to people bearing wisdom. We are introspective and are constantly trying to make ourselves better (in addition to making the world better) so when someone new comes along looking like a *teacher* or someone who is trying to lead a better life, we can be easily fooled. Only upon our deliberate effort to slow down and observe the person's actions can we realize that his memorization of lofty and spiritual quotes does not mean he is living that wisdom. Open people must learn to develop their observational skills.

Since yoga has recently become a popular fad, and many Empaths are drawn to its healing benefits, we must be careful because predators are drawn to the same healing fields. Predators are drawn toward soft and healing people and places to find their own safety and healing as well. Yes, Narcissists innately know they are injured but they lack the ability to stop the hell that lives inside of them. They live their lives feeling fragmented and they are constantly seeking not only an Empath to fulfill them, but places and activities that bring them a sense of wholeness. And with Yoga Teaching

Certificates now so quick and easy to achieve, some ego-driven people are becoming yoga teachers.

Empaths must start using wisdom nature for discernment in their better protection. Operating heart-center is a beautiful and evolved quality but we must first ensure our own protection before we open ourselves to others that may be harmful.

Pets

Just like we are an object to stimulate The Narcissist, so is his pet. Narcissists need and crave sensory stimulation and that is why many of them are cheaters, sex addicts, voracious eaters, and have other addictions. They are sensory deadened and require extreme amounts of sensory input to be able to absorb the impressions. My Sociopath went crazy with delight when smelling his cat and rubbing its fur all over his face, but he didn't care if the poor critter had clean water or if it was safe in the house away from coyotes. Narcissists crave touch, or tactile stimulation, like we all do, but to a compulsive level. Again, this is craving a Mother's Essence of touch.

My Sociopath bathed my two small dogs in strong perfumy-smelling shampoo. From the moment immediately after their bath to about 24 hours later, he "loved" my dogs. Other than these 24-hour periods of the strong shampoo smell, he hated my dogs and threatened to kill them, especially the male dog if he came to me for attention. My Sociopath was only "lovingly" responding to an intense olfactory stimulation of the perfume smell...not the poor dogs. (You may notice that your socio/narc/bpd has to have the intense chemical smell of dryer sheets on all his laundry to feel as if things are clean).

An Open person bonds with animals and all of nature on a higher, more spiritual level. We feel a connection to animals and innately understand that all lives intertwine. If we hurt, so too does the animals. If we suffer when hungry or cold, so too does the neglected and uncared for animals. We want to be loved, taken care of and in a safe place; so too does all living creatures. The Narcissist is unable to feel the spiritual flow of nature and its creatures; he is disconnected. It is ironic, however, that The Narcissist will make us feel that we are somehow defective in our higher spiritual connection to the earth and animals and we will squash this part of ourselves to conform to his more low-level needs.

Turk Narc told me that I only cared about the animals because I was abused as a child. He made me believe in my innate badness for loving animals. I was attacked at one of the many Turk Narc's parties when I was in my 20s, and everyone else was 40s through 60s, *for taking care of the animals instead of the orphaned or sick children in the hospitals.* However, when I nicely replied in return, "Are you taking care of the sick and orphaned children?" I was attacked even further because my attacker was doing no such thing. In fact, I was indeed taking care of the "sick" children as well: I was a Special Education teacher that was taking my neglected students out to special events and dinners with my own money.

Our spiritual flow expands everywhere. A Narcissist is spiritually constricted and only appears to spiritually flow when someone is stimulating him.

The main component that keeps a Narcissist supported: Drama!

1. **Narcissist Drama:** When he is feeling deprived of the spotlight, he will cry of some severe sickness, personal dilemma (his own problem or the "crazy" partner or ex situation), or create an enemy of the group.

2. **Narcissist Family and Friend Drama:** He will exaggerate something that happens to a family member or friend and will call out his forces with his cries and woes begging for their support.

3. **The Grand Gesture King:** He will forget about family and "friends" but if one of these has a crisis or is planning a special event, he will run to the scene and be the Grand Gesture King. He will go overboard and be the one that shines. For example: He ignores his

friend, barely knows his sister, the sister dies and The Narcissist will run to the friend and be the Great Saver. He will even go so far as to help in the planning of her memorial service. Shouldn't her family be doing that? However, unthinking "friends" will fall for this fair-weather-friend and his run-to-the-rescue appearance even though he let this "friend" down many times before during his less dramatic situations. The Grand Gesture King is the hero at parties, hospitals and funeral scenes.

Part Two...Childhood

FIVE

THE ABUSED CHILD'S REALITY DISTORTION

If someone wants to listen to me, if someone seems as if they are interested in me, I will talk...I will spill out all the thoughts in my inner-dwelling place so any nearby predator can penetrate my vulnerabilities. I don't understand that humanity contains evilness. If I do get a hint of danger, I dismiss it as my own misunderstanding; I don't trust my own intelligent mind that is trying to intuitively lead me out of harm and into safety. I have been working on improving this weakness for the past two-years...during the writing of these words. Writing has helped me greatly in aligning more with intelligence and intuition and reacting less to emotions or to those who manipulate and pull my heart-strings. (I can't tell you how many joyful, peaceful, as well as challenging days, I spent working on these writings instead of hanging out with a bad man...goals are life saving.)

If you lived in my childhood home, you would think that I would end up the opposite or have a great understanding that monsters exist. When others tell me about their abusive, neglectful parent, it seems they always shine brightness into the story by explaining with a reminiscent smile, "But my mother (or father or grandmother) was my light, my savior, she (he) held us all together." I wish I were so lucky to have at least one loving parent and/or relative; both my parents were emotionally out-of-control and my brothers and I were scared and bewildered rag-dolls. When a child comes out of this home, where all is crazy and there is no understanding of proper human behavior, she will accept anything from anyone and confuse the showing up of anyone in her life that offers her attention, or even a meal, as love.

When I was 16-years-old, my father shouted "Bitter Sixteen" at me as I came within his view. He named all the happy neighborhood girls smiling and having "Sweet Sixteen" birthday parties. I would NOT have a 16th birthday celebration; I never had a birthday party, ever. Neither did I ever experience a happy Christmas or Thanksgiving, or any holiday. My mother told me that she never had a birthday party so it was no big deal; *only spoiled brats had birthday parties.* This is The Narcissist changing reality and the time-line or twisting the sequence of events (gaslighting): I was raised scared, so I would be taunted for being "bitter," therefore, I would not have a "Sweet Sixteen" party because I was "bitter," though, I never had a birthday party before and only spoiled brats had them anyway. I was in no way honored as a "Sweet Sixteen" girl; I was made into a scared child and then punished for it. This is a Narcissist's brain projected into the forming nucleus of their child's permanent wiring system that creates a sociopath/narcissist, empath or a basket-case; a child that hates him/herself and will harm themselves, or allow others to harm them, or be the one that harms.

My mother and father did not attend the high school graduation of their children. To this day, I am not allowed to speak of my MA with my mother; she gets angry and shuts me off in mid-sentence because I am "bragging." My father never knew I graduated with a BA, let alone an MA. I feel as if I never accomplished anything though many documents say I did. I feel disconnected from my achievements...as if it wasn't really me that did the work. I don't feel or act like an educated person. After Turk Narc Professor, I congregated toward poor and uneducated male lovers and female friends. I always maintained civility with my parents across the country and rarely mentioned anything positive about myself because I believed in my low-level life. I was not only a loser at 18, but continued to be one no matter the years that passed, my accomplishments, or the degrees I received. I can see my parents' mental illness and I can understand it through the Universe of Humanity and Compassion (well, sometimes I can; it's hard to be a "big person" all the time), so I quietly dismiss their inability to evolve. I survive by thinking the New Age blurb of, "If they could have done better, they would have."

My father died a few years ago and I never once expressed an angry word to him. I have to be this way; if I express anger, I am called "crazy." Narcissists and Sociopaths drive their children and their lovers to anguish and when we break down in hurt, they switch to eerie calm and now have an upper-hand over our display of beaten-down emotional expression. This is a sign of sociopath abuse and needs to be understood in the field of psychology and in the mental health and court systems.

No matter the chaos they create, Sociopaths and Narcissists switch their emotions to radiate cool and calm.

When a person is displaying signs of frazzled emotions or emotional fatigue...when their loved one is showing cool, detached emotionalism...this could be a red flag that the cold and detached person is the "crazy" one and not vice-versa. Look at it this way: Who can stay cold and detached when another person is hurting? We live in a World of Opposites: I can, with a low voice, a bit smiley, showing no emotionalism, tell someone to *Go Fuck Off* and I would likely be seen as normal. Yet, if I screamed at a person about the injuries they inflicted upon me and my life, I would be considered "crazy." In truth, a healthy expression of emotionalism is good...emotional detachment and vacancy after harming someone is sociopathic. The court system in the United States plays this game of opposites: The abuser is cool and calm while the abused is frazzled. Thence, the emotionally detached person is given the benefit of the doubt whereas the emotionally broken person is dismissed as not credible. The emotional person (within limits and appropriate to the situation) is actually the one manifesting more normalcy and credibility.

THE ABUSED CHILD'S REALITY DISTORTION

Narcissists and Sociopaths have fits of rage that they effectively conceal behind portraying another person as bad, wrong, or crazy. Their fits of rage happen because someone said something to them that goes against their portrayal of a superior human-being and thus, their ego is damaged. We ceased to be our accommodating, complimenting and accepting selves and we crossed into the protective boundaries of the mentally-ill or personality disturbed and we upset them. This was our fault that he had the rage attack because we were bad and said something about a harm he was causing. Sociopaths cannot take any sort of "criticism," even though they are creating the concerning issue. When we fail to quietly accept their harmful actions, and try to defend our boundaries, we become the "abuser."

However, my father didn't need words to set his ego off into a rage; it felt attacked and insulted for just about everything. It was my father's tradition to have a rage-fit on Christmas and Thanksgiving. These holidays were *special* for him because they represented *love and family* more than say Halloween or Fourth of July. Father would create a huge fight with my mother, physically and verbally assault all of us, and then retreat to his bedroom. My mother would sit, sob, and mutter, "I wish he were dead," as the three of us opened our Christmas gifts. There was never music in my childhood home; no Christmas music; no special sounds at all. This rage-fit and "I wish he were dead" muttering was my family's special holiday record; it spun for 18-years straight.

Thanksgiving was even more Sociopath Special. As my grandparents and aunts drove up the driveway, father would turn bright red, run and hide in his bedroom...staying there the entire day. My parents' bedroom had dark brown drapes that were always closed, mustard colored painted walls and blood red carpet. This was the den of the hiding sociopath father. Our house had no soul, no spirit, no light...all windows painted shut. I remember being punished for trying to pry my bedroom window open; I wasn't even allowed to part the drapes. The family members driving up on Thanksgiving were HIS parents and sisters. My mother told me that he hated his family. Looking back now, could my mother have cast her own sociopath energy into the dynamics of this family to create even more stress and conflict?

To this day, I don't celebrate Christmas or Thanksgiving and barely acknowledge my birthday. If I should attend a Christmas gathering at someone's home it is a strange sight for me to see happy and loving people gathered together. I don't like to tell anyone the day of my birth because it makes me feel uncomfortable when this day comes and it is recognized.

The rules of my childhood home changed every day. Actually, rules did not exist because rule-making would require a 'family.' Nothing was ever planned: It was chaos and war. My parents were one team, though it didn't seem like it, and the children were on the opposing side with no concept or understanding of what the rules of this adult game were. In our young minds it was normal for parents to hate their children because we were bad.

I still feel that I am bad, though I've never really done anything bad. I attract bad believing this is my worth and if I fix the bad, I will be worthy.

My mother taught me: *All people are crazy. Sure, Mrs. Beadle across the street seems happy; she is the mother of five seemingly happy children and a wife of a solid and apparently content man. But Mrs. Beadle is inwardly screaming because she hates her children, her home, her family; she wants to be alone...to be free. Everyone hates one another, everyone hates their children and family and everyone should live on their own island.* When my brothers or I approached my mother with a hurt or a question, she hissed at us, *I wish you were dead.* When my father was in a rage, she mumbled to us, *I wish he were dead,* and even more often, *I wish I were dead.* My mother threatened suicide on a regular basis. Each step down the school bus and up the driveway, my insides filled with terror and my head formulated a clear picture: My mother dead...in her own blood...because I was bad.

My mother never touched me once I grew out of infancy. She never showed me makeup or nail polish and never brushed my hair. I was bathing and dressing myself at 3 years old. Instead, my mother taught me that people are similar to cockroaches. I never had a conversation with either of my parents...it was all *People are Bad* talk. She told me that a person only has a child because of their obsession with duplicating their own image and when they realize their cute baby has grown out of his/her cuteness and is now a screaming, demanding, feces and throw-up making, individual thinking and acting entity, the parent hates the child and wishes he/she was never born. My mother made me believe that her and my father were the norm with their explosive and hateful destruction toward their family and every other family was only presenting a fake image of love. Despite this talk, I yearned to be loved.

I smiled and waved goodbye to my parents to drive across the country with a man that I just met. When I turned 18, my father yelled at me that I was too old to live in his home, and in fact, I was just too old and hadn't accomplished anything in life; I was a loser and my name thenceforth became "Loser." He started charging me $250.00/rent; a lot of money for an 18 year old, in the mid '80s, living in a small room in a screaming house filled with hate. This same year, the year I turned 18, my aunt bought me black balloons with white lettering that read "Over The Hill." I remember being embarrassed of not only how old I was, but that I ended up being a nobody on my 18th birthday.

Keith, my kitty Cashmere, and I arrived in California and I was *saved* from my life as an *Old 18 year old* in a small town in Ohio. Soon after, I was living in Barstow and married to my first Sociopath. I immediately went to work and on one of these workdays, Cashmere was to be spayed. Keith took her to the vet and had her euthanized instead. As I inquired about her pick-up time, he explained to me, as I stood frozen, that it was done because she opened the cupboard doors at night. Any resilient Spirit that assisted me in my childhood and guided me away from my ugly family home, was now dimmed and far away from me as I was now a tragic outline of what was supposed to be a human being; my essence crumbled into a pile outside myself.

THE ABUSED CHILD'S REALITY DISTORTION

I entered the world of grownups far away from *home*, on the opposite side of our country, and in order to survive, I was open to anything, anyone, everything, everyone. I assumed all people were normal when being crazy. If someone did a horrible act against me, and I cried with despair, and they told me that I was wrong, I believed them. This led to my ingrained belief that I had to accept crazy wrapped up in eerie calmness because if I reacted, then I would be the true mentally ill. I wouldn't be *perfect*, I would be that *Bitter Sixteen*. I lived life attracting predators and they intuitively knew that I was scared into portraying perfect so they exploited this insecurity...pushed me to my limits and when I reacted, I was the defective; I was *Crazy, Crazy just like my parents. We* remain accepting far too long and then release a red vortex of our hidden emotions. Ultimately, we retreat back into quiet acceptance once again because we are afraid there will be consequences for our making a stand.

I called my mother crying and explained to her what happened and she matter-of-factly stated, "That didn't happen." My world did another flip-flop: She is my mother, she loves me, she is right. Those were the days when a girl believed in not only her mother's love but her mother's truth. My mother continued to explain that Cashmere was sick and Keith did the right thing. "But...Cashmere wasn't sick"....as my voice trailed softly away...I silently said in my head, "it was cupboards..." I didn't want to upset my mother. I was wrong; I didn't know anything even though it happened in front of my eyes and my mother was 2,500 miles away. My mother was the truth, I was a lie; my existence was bad; Cashmere died because of me.

I believed in my mother and in this Sociopath. I would leave this man, doubt my perceptions of the horrendous act he executed, and then I would return to him. This is a typical cycle of an Empath living among her Sociopaths and Narcissists: They destroy us; we doubt reality due to their brainwashing. They convince us of their perfect and all-knowing knowledge, and their more self-assured and directed personalities dominate over our more gentle and yielding souls. We are programmed by the Narcissist's gaslighting and their projected grandiosity and animated perfection...we are weak, inferior, and wrong. We, The Open, rarely trust our perceptions. We are trusting and believe in people's good even when their bad destroys us.

I always felt as if I were floating along in an air-stream. This feeling of being ungrounded led me into a series of relationships based upon perceptions and decisions that were not solid: I allowed things to happen to me. This is why I so easily return to bad relationships. I never believed in my experiences but only in what others told me MY experiences were. I permitted anyone to enter my space, violate me, and to remain in my presence.

Cashmere was never brought up again until now, all these years later, as I write these words: My mother, now 71-years-old, just screamed at me on the phone, "Look what you did to Keith. You were horrible to him. Keith never killed Cashmere, she was sick!" Twenty-five years later the wicked sting of a sick mother still penetrates with venom to my very core. First time in my entire life, I am refusing to answer her calls and texts. I finally walked away. I still have moments where I feel that I am wrong...wrong in everything that I do, that I see, that I perceive. Now, I fight with thoughts that I am wrong in not speaking with her.

Narcissistic mothers look out for everyone but their own children. Indeed, abusers DO have empathy, just not for the right people and especially not for their children or the people they are supposed to look out for. By having empathy for sources that are not of priority, Narcissists keep themselves emotionally safe.

The most important emotional connection of my life, the one person who was to protect my body, mind, and spirit, told me things that happened, didn't happen...a baby formed into an adult by A Mother Gaslighter. Children have a chance of surviving and healing from a father's physical beatings and from a mother's cold, emotional detachment. However, when moulded into being by gaslighting you are left fighting the deep, emotional essence of living a wrong existence.

People who commit suicide do so after years, decades, of fighting their belief in their wrong existence. Those who grow up in families where it was instilled within them that they are solid and right in their life and perceptions, therefore, right in their existence, will be less likely to commit suicide when life-issues present themselves (unless there is a chemical imbalance).

Those that are raised validated survive life.

For those of us from troubled childhood homes and terrible parents, we turn into shamed humans. When we are grown and raised in a family that diminishes us, we project this shame through all our decisions, actions, and relationships. When we are older and in a bad relationship, or in another bad relationship, we think through clouds of unworthiness that it is our fault and we must fix what is wrong. Children that are raised in good, solid, loving homes, don't blame themselves when someone disrespects them, crosses their boundaries, or acts untrustworthy or disloyal: Un-shamed Children turn into adults that are self-assured and clear in their perceptions of wrong treatment and can walk away at the first sign of red flags. Shamed Children cannot properly process the things that people do to them and have difficulty in accurately understanding what goes on around them. They give bad people credit because bad people are the aggressors of the world and are masters at creating an illusion of rightful assertiveness and all-knowing knowledge.

The Shamed Adult will stay and/or constantly return to the abuser because they blame themselves for overreacting or misunderstanding bad actions from others or they believe all relationships are filled with drama, disloyalty, manipulations and pain and it is something that they must be more accommodating toward and understanding of. We may initially react appropriately against the mistreatment (shouts; leaving) but will soon retreat back into shame and doubt and return to the abuser. The Shamed are programmed to believe that they are the wrong, the bad, the exaggerating, the too sensitive. Predators see and migrate to this type of programming because the self-assured and grounded person with solid ideals and perceptions would not be controlled or manipulated. The Narcissist thrives off the shame and doubt of others. He preys upon targets who get easily confused, lack direction, are naively trusting and give repeated chances.

Because everything seems to go wrong in the Empath's relationships, their difficulty in grounding themselves worsens and they stumble downhill even more. It becomes cyclical: Empaths draw in dark forces to their light and these dark forces dampen their light.

Evaluate why you do not have clear insight regarding right and wrong, good and bad, healthy and unhealthy; why you let things go too far and why you may be too forgiving. Start training yourself to think intellectually instead of emotionally. This means stopping before jumping into situations that are not beneficial, but also recognizing when to act quickly upon good opportunities that may expand your life. This requires brain-training; only allowing high-quality items of merit to enter your consciousness.

A few of my personal suggestions:

- **Read higher-level materials:** *I'm reading philosophy by the ancient wisdom writers.*

- **Learn new and more advanced skills:** *I'm studying how to draw sacred geometry symbols using a compass and protractor.*

- **Avoid low-level and negative TV, movies and social media:** *I watch documentaries on YouTube, talks on TED Talks, heartfelt comedies on movie channels,* and *listen to NPR Radio. I only write educational material on social media and avoid interacting in meaningless ways.*

- **Organize your home and finances** *so that you have a clear view into your environment and its needs.*

SIX

TAKING AWAY OUR IMAGE AND BEING

Looking back at my 1980's childhood, it seems that humans of then are not the same humans of current. Parents now live in fear of their children and two-decades ago, this was not the case. If my childhood home existed today, it would be taken down by a SWAT team. I know not to speak of this to others because if I express concern over their hurting or betraying me, or their lying or unfair acts, it would be manipulated against me that I am defective from childhood and that my perceptions are wrong. I will be spun into a ball of another's making. I've learned this lesson over and over...

Not only this, but by 24-years-old, I already divorced an abusive man and when I narrated some of these details with those of my childhood, I was perceived as the central character in not only a sob story, but a bad story. People take more liberties with weak forces than with strong forces. Add to this that a short time ago personality disorders were not so widely known about, especially their traumatic effects upon others, and a woman who talked of abuse was thought to be an exaggerator. This can still be present day case, but overall, there is more awareness that predator personalities exist and cause psychological damage to their victims.

The first relationship after my young, runaway marriage was with a much older Professor and he could treat me anyway he wanted. One of the ways in which he got away with this was he maintained cool and calm and sent me into reaction mode. I believed in my inferiority to him and this not-good-enough feeling came largely because I was out-of-control emotionally when in a relationship with him. He made me highly reactive and anxious; he even walked paces in front of me as I panted and struggled to keep up with him. He taunted me that I was *Like my mother.* Narcissist use our family and what we reveal to them against us.

Turk Narc proclaimed to come from "Greatness" and I was cracked and damaged goods. Subconsciously I was looking for a family, someone to take care of me, and I ended up not only taking care of myself during this precarious time of life, but made sure the needs of an older, well established Turkish Professor that hailed from "Ottoman Greatness," was first and foremost in my young-adulthood struggling life. I was 25 and he was 40. I just made it through college while working, doing animal rescue work, keeping my own apartment, and living across the country from any family; yet, I had to be it all, do it all for Turk Narc.

Old souls, though young in human years, end up catering to the demands of older people who should be protecting the younger.

After a long trail of culminating events where proper human boundaries were crossed, or what should have been my boundaries, I hid away from Turk Narc for a few days, saying nothing, and in the worst case, I threw the glass-encased picture of us to the patio ground. He held the latter against me for decades as his evidence that I was crazy: *She screamed and broke a picture:* He told everyone, everywhere; it preceded me as I awkwardly walked into Turkish Parties filled with people 20-years my senior. I was encrusted in a cloak of my *mother's craziness.* No matter how much I educated myself, no matter how many animals I rescued, no matter how many times I forgave Turk Narc for cheating and lying, I was *Crazy* because I smashed the picture. Sociopaths and Narcissists use our normal reactions to human violations and the things we share with them about our family, about ourselves...to overshadow us with their power. We spend our lives as their hostages.

I was about 9-years-old and learning to play the clarinet in school. I was proud that I learned "When The Saints Go Marching In." I took that clarinet in front of my parents who were sitting in the living room and played my great accomplishment to them. When I finished, I stood and smiled. They both remained looking at the TV. Not a word was ever said. I walked back to my room and silently put my clarinet away.

I recently told my mother what I discovered about My Sociopath and that I was now writing about it. She told me that *all this sociopath stuff is nonsense and my father was diagnosed a sociopath long ago, and it's no big deal.* I was always told my father went into a facility when I was a baby in the 1970s to dry out from his alcoholism. Turns out alcoholism was involved but it was only a component of my father's more serious mental illness. My mother boasted that *long ago, when no one used the "sociopath" word, she knew what it meant because the people in my father's hospital diagnosed him as one*; and she (my mother) was *one of the first people to be associated with the "sociopath" term, so who cares, no big deal.* She continued that *I was not the first person to throw the "sociopath" word around thinking that I was smart and better than everyone else. In fact, the young woman psychologist randomly threw it at my father to show-off her education.* My mother explained that *the "sociopath" word is just "psychobabble" nonsense, and people in the mental health field use this word against people as a label to make themselves and their profession seem proficient and competent.*

I learned during these writings that my father was at Massillon; known as Massillon State Hospital for The Insane until the 1970s. It was established in 1892 as the first state hospital in the US and Canada and was originally named Eastern Ohio Mental Asylum.

Well, that explains so much. No wonder I spent my life seeking the protection of older narcissistic and sociopathic men. I was raised by one! My mother was calm and humorous as she told me this shocking detail; yet she had emotional fits of rage when my brothers and I had tiny squabbles as children. This is typical of someone with a personality disorder: They can sit calmly as the roof caves in but they can't tolerate the sounds of children.

My mother's voice and tone was light as she explained this surreal information to the daughter of a sociopath that spent her adult life loving and being destroyed by sociopathic men; as if it were a normal and everyday thing and *All men are wrongly diagnosed as sociopaths.* My mother fed her children illusions from her delusions. I am now unscrambling my mother's participation in the cruelty toward her children, when all my life, I thought she too was a victim. She is still taking no responsibility for, and even denying, the ruination of many generations of our family; she lives in complete disconnect. She ruined her generation: All my family hates one another and are in conflict because of her negative energy between us all; she destroyed the generation that came after her, her own children; and now my suffering brothers have weakened children, her grandchildren. When the seeds of mental illness are planted, they bloom forth for generations.

Her presence suffocated our soul, and its contemptuous doubt boiled about our spirit, dragging us into the depths of her miserable existence (Szepes, 250).

As another story goes and as my mother tells it with a sparkle: I was 2-years-old and rocking in my small, wooden rocking chair that was facing a corner. As I rocked forward, I threw up, as I rocked back, I smiled...Even at 2, I didn't want to be a burden. My mother thought I had the flu and ignored this strange and tiny thing rocking and throwing up in a corner. My Aunt Eleanor walked in and rushed me to the hospital as my mother persisted that I had the flu. I spent weeks in ICU because of a ruptured appendix. My mother tells me to this day that I was a good baby for not crying while dying. This same rocking chair now sits in a corner of my home and I can see it as I write. *At least my family has a good sense of humor.*

As a result, I had a long vertical scar going up the right, lower quadrant of my belly that would progressively indent and attach to muscle with a pucker. As a 16 year old insecure, shell of a girl, I was forced into a bikini by my father to prominently display this horrible mess of mangled abdomen. Father forced me to cut the grass of our front lawn with a push mower, in that bikini, with that scar gleaming in the unforgiving sun to show all the neighbors that I wasn't shy. Being shamed for being shy, being shamed for my mother's scars, being shamed for being alive.

I can shove aside this memory, and many similar to it, but the swirling and haunting images of my mind will never be subdued when it comes to my brother. Empaths can set aside the violent and cutting acts inflicted upon their own souls, but they cannot dismiss similar mistreatments toward others. We disregard our own injuries but we see and feel the soul hurts of others. My older brother was 17 and when image was everything for not only our own soul survival but for our survival within the group, on a random and sporadic schedule, my father forced him to submerge his hands into a giant jar of Vaseline and swab his own hair with this thick petroleum jelly. He was then forced to get on the school bus to a shocked bus driver and jeering young riders as my father stood looking on from the top of our driveway, belted jeans, no shirt, arms crossed over an exposed belly covered with black hair. When other 17 year olds were happily driving themselves and friends to school, my brother sat on a school bus weighed down in Vaseline wearing my father's heavy burden.

My brother learned to be a class clown...to be the one that was funny and not the one hated by a sociopath 'father.' This wasn't even his real father and I could only believe that his real father would have loved him. Those who smile the brightest, joke and laugh the most, and are the most accepting of others, are often the most injured.

Sociopaths do not want us to light up because to them, our shine means we stand outside and away and independent from their vast inner darkness, loneliness and isolation. When they take us away from our spirit's light, when our soul retreats into hiding, when our personality operates to make them 'happy,' then they are temporarily satiated and slightly removed from their emptiness. Sociopaths control our light because they can't generate their own. Having your own light scares him because he is fearful someone else will notice it and that you will leave him. Dousing of your light is for his survival.

I don't know if I'll ever fully recover from sociopath abuse but I will learn to survive the best way that I can by using creative expression to reach out to the world. We recover through expansion. Being here, now, writing these words, is the only relief that I get so that I can continue to function in a world that allows innocent humans and animals to be destroyed. The suffering stays inside of us unless it is used for positive.

A Sociopath will see you as unapproachable if you maintain who you are and what you want in life. This is having a solid sense of self and it is built through positive work and creation and improving one's own environment and living conditions. Sociopaths look for those who operate through personality or the intense need to be loved, approved of and accepted (just like the sociopath himself) and this comes out through our accepting him and his manic relationship just so we don't have to be alone. He absorbs those who readily sacrifice their soul expression to seek satisfaction in a world of his shallow senses. Sociopaths are deterred by those who express their personality through their soul; those who radiate soul through staying on their own path without drifting onto someone else's. They veer away from focused people who do not succumb to whims.

SEVEN

THE UNDERDOG ELEMENT

The Narcissist And The Underdog

If my mother and I talked about how bad someone was doing, all went well. If I talked emotionally about something terrible a man did to me, she would feel empathy for my abuser and hiss at me that I was a liar or exaggerator or got the facts wrong. Narcissists do not see their children as emotional beings but mere physical objects, therefore, they cannot connect to our emotional expressions and may even become angry and frustrated as a result (shallow affect). No matter how bad a man turned out to be, my mother believed that I should stay with him and work *It* out; *it was the practical thing to do because life was bad anyway and I shouldn't make an issue out of abuse.*

Narcissists find their loved ones the easiest targets of abuse; they do not feel empathy for their children, or a devoted spouse or family member, but will feel empathy toward an abuser that they see as the "misunderstood." Less emotional energy and mental thought is required to support an abuser. However, an emotional connection is needed when supporting an abuse-victim and Narcissists are incapable of this. My mother went so far as to tell me that those who claim abuse by their parents are spoiled and are having a tantrum because they're not getting their way. She told me that any woman claiming rape was lying. This brainwashing instilled a sense of guilt in her children down to a mind-control level that if we mentioned abuse, we were not only liars, but spoiled. Create human-shells out of children by conditioning them that if they should even think, let alone say, that they are hurting, they are bad. The child goes on to live a life full of guilt, fear and shame whereas The Narcissistic parent is free from worry and responsibility.

My mother believed that marriage or an intimate partnership was for convenience or financial reasons; this led her to accept a bad man that destroyed her children. And as long as her children were fed, clothed, and housed while young (and in their adult relationships), despite being beaten and tortured, all was fine.

When I was older, and still attempting to go to my mother about something bad that happened to me, she would repeat a funny, white lie that I told in middle school as proof that I was nothing but a liar. Narcissists live in a warped frame of reference regarding time. Since they do not attach emotionally, they attach to physical representations of a certain fixed point in their child's life, and this is usually when the child was young and before they formed and expressed their own opinions and clear emotional thoughts. In a way, we were more *under-doggish* when we were younger, as opposed to when we become adults. Narcissists try to keep their children emotionally and mentally at 10-years-old.

My mother has no other photos of me but my required high school graduation picture. She displays it prominently: My 1980's big hair, matted with hairspray, and blue-pencil eyeliner pressed into my lower-lids. Just recently, I sent her a current picture of me and her response was, "Who's that?"

If I mention another person receiving unconditional love from their family, my mother screams at me and calls me names. I tested this typical reaction many times and would say, "Janie has a great family." I knew that I was inciting her but it was so bizarre of a scene, that I felt compelled to do this anyway in the hope of shaking her into reality. I wanted her to tell me that I didn't get what I needed, but I deserved all the love in the world...I wanted this so that I could start healing. You will never receive apologies from abusers because this inability to take responsibility and to self-reflect is what makes them abusive to begin with. I, on the other hand, emotionally bear the burden of things that I'm not even responsible for.

My mother flies into a rage if I mention Janie and her family because there is no underdog in this home. It is a strong family made of love. I grew up in a middle-class neighborhood and attended one of the better school districts in the area. There was one street that overlapped into this fine school district and it was of dilapidated, tiny shacks and people of extreme poverty. Monica, in my same class, lived on this street. She was called "Dirty Monica" because she came to school covered in dirt. Her hair was matted to her head with grease and she wore torn clothes and shoes with holes. I told my mother of this girl and she went into action. Every school play, picnic, or event, my mother picked up Monica and forced us to attend together. At the time, I was mortified, but just a couple years later, I sought out my own 'Monicas.'

My mother taking care of Monica is a nice gesture but not when she and my father were destroying their own children. **Narcissists do have empathy but it plays alongside Emotional Obsession.** They are incapable of measured, emotional attachments with appropriate people that is of a steadfast and consistent nature but will instead seek inappropriate emotional distractions that are Obsessive. Their Emotional Obsessions rotate quickly through all sorts of people and some of these people appear out of nowhere.

Narcissists have Emotionally Obsessive relationships.

The Empath And The Underdog

A pattern starts in middle school where we congregate toward the misunderstood kids. We start fighting for, defending, and relating to the underdog at a young age. Not all underdogs or "misunderstoods" are Narcissists, but certain categories of people have more drama in their life. We easily connect to those misplaced in society because this is how we feel deep down about ourselves. In addition, we try to help those less fortunate or less understood because this is what we want and crave for ourselves.

THE UNDERDOG ELEMENT

Middle school is also the time that we start feeling that everyone can SEE that we are *damaged goods*. We believe our scars are transparent to everyone and we enter into a self-sabotaging mode of operation. I would often verbalize my *defectiveness* because I believed that others saw it anyway; we think our wounds are visible, that we are different, so we behave as if we are different. Narcissists are attracted to those who reveal and self-deprecate; we are like open sores to them. Many of us never outgrow this feeling of transparency. For me, there was a bit of truth to this feeling of visible shame.

The neighbors heard the guns going off in my childhood home. My mother shot through a bathroom door at my father. He was not hit but remained silent and crouching behind the ceramic sink that he used as a shield to deflect the bullets. Because he remained quiet, my mother thought he was dead and called for an ambulance. When the ambulance arrived, my father came smiling out of the bathroom. We all went out to dinner after the police situation was handled, and my mother was aglow that my father had entered his *nice spell* after she attempted to gun him down during one of his terrorizing tantrums. The memories of this day remained the same throughout my childhood and this shot-up house was recently sold with the same bullet-holes covered by rose stickers.

Empaths, especially those abused in childhood, are conditioned that people will let us down, so we congregate toward a *lower-status* person with the feeling that the misunderstood will not only accept us, but see us as their *leader*. Empaths have powerful qualities, and make positive leaders, if given the right circumstances and environment; herein lies our problem: we instead gravitate toward soul sucking situations.

Middle school is also the age where we pull back from any friend(s) that we still have from our younger years that come from more settled and loving environments. We believe that we no longer fit into normalcy and have a feeling of misplacement. This is the time that we feel as if we are adopted, actually we hope that we are, or even that we are from another planet. We start becoming hypersensitive and sabotage somewhat healthier relationships. We stop getting along in school and see teachers as our enemies and are no longer academically motivated.

The brightest abused children fall through the cracks in middle school because no one wants to deal with their behaviors...their overt behaviors or their self-sabotaging and retreating behaviors. I went from the top of my elementary school to acting out in middle school to sleeping in or skipping classes in high school. In high school, the craziest girl in school (destructive and dangerous crazy) liked me and I was flattered. Her high energy intrigued me and I believed that I was special because her wild mania chose me. Because I wasn't too overtly damaging, only quietly and inwardly damaging, I was ignored by the adults and left to disappear within the system. I tried to quietly commit suicide during these years: I drank shampoo and this made my parents laugh. I tried to disappear by being anorexic and the more underweight I went, the cuter my parents and others thought me to be. I was the type of student that needed to be out of the traditional public schools and put into a school for the creative arts.

In reality, people don't see us as *damaged goods*...then or now. Because we are suffering, we force an outer smile and are very friendly. We are the ones that show and tell people that we think lowly of ourselves. We reveal this mainly through tolerating bad people and their damaging behaviors and self-deprecating talk. In actuality, as we grow older and emerge from schooling, we become brighter, more smiley in appearance, charismatic (not narcissist attention-seeking charismatic but genuinely) and more giving because we had to grow-up quickly. We realize that we must mask our pain to fit into society; to manage in the world of intimate relationships, work, and societal obligations. We see and understand the pains of the world and those around us at an early age and we yearn to compassionately bond with others...we just don't know how to do this and we don't know how to find the right people to do it with.

Because of our kind soul, we attract good people in our lives but we cannot sustain these relationships. We invest more of our time and energy in keeping the personality disordered and mentally disturbed (*the underdog*) in our lives happy and complacent because they are more of a challenge and we wrongly believe: If we gain their love and acceptance... subsequently, we are okay. And these emotionally-detached people remind us more of our upbringing and are a more comfortable fit for us. The personality disordered people-please us in the beginning of the relationship and this brings us comfort and healing; we in turn reciprocate or people-please double back, allowing them to manipulate our time away.

We have Emotionally Obsessive relationships just like The Narcissist. Being a kind person is a great thing but this does not mean allowing ourselves to be destroyed. We must look inward and make adjustments.

The better people in our lives are lost because we put an inordinate amount of our energy into pleasing The Narcissist at the disposal of other people with our last-minute canceling of plans and not returning their calls and invitations. This is a red flag of someone with a personality disorder: no regard for our friends, plans and commitments. There is also the fact that Narcissists warp our feelings toward the other people in our lives and they do covert things behind our back with these people to turn us against them, and them against us. As we grow older, good people are harder for us to find...and we burned bridges trying to satiate Narcissists and Sociopaths. We even start looking like we are the ones who have the mental health issues. In the end, only bad people are available to us.

Our lives become a cycle of being drawn to underdogs, knowing that we are good and deserve more, to finding healthier people that genuinely enjoy us, to losing these better relationship because we find ourselves investing every ounce of our being into giving sociopath attention and trying to satiate his insatiable ego, to having nothing and no one left in the end.

A Narcissist creates such a nervous relationship that we think we must be constantly in his presence or he will find someone new. His entire existence is of such Unbearable Loneliness that we are never safe.

After divorcing My Sociopath, I thought I was smart about bad people...I now know what a Sociopath is. Understanding your life pattern, knowing what a sociopath is, does not make you bullet-proof from letting one enter your life again. We attract them on an emotional level, not an intellectual one. The first man that I attracted after My Sociopath was a raging alcoholic with either narcissism or borderline personality disorder. I tried to *save* him. People with personality disorders see our wounds and our openness and swoop down on us while we are weakened...despite fooling ourselves that we are strong.

Until we can emotionally process our lives, our patterns, find closure with our past difficulties...until we develop emotional strength along with our intellectual power...we will continue to attract clones of our former abusers. You must evaluate not only your thinking and judgment skills, but your emotional behaviors. Are you emotionally attracted to unavailable people? Are you a "saver?" Are you pulled in by the underdog energy (those living on the fringes; those misunderstood)? Are you attracted to bad men (women)?

Take control of your life through ACTION:

You must process your childhood, your history of attracting abuse, but this processing must take place both emotionally and intellectually, and then you must take action for the development of new habits that don't trap you into emotional chattering and emotional behaviors. This comes through action, from moving and doing, from exercising, from working and toiling on the earth and with the animals, and in the line of service work. (Picking weeds was a form of meditation for me during the peak of sociopath devastation.)

Dwell within the Science of Service. Volunteer for the earth, animals, children, abused, sick, elderly. You must engage in service work that emanates from your soul, or genuine love for all life, and not service work that you feel obligated toward or you think will make you look good. When you see soul in others, when you respond to their soul with your soul, you are on the path to not only healing yourself, but others. We find ourselves through others.

It is called a "Science" because it has been proven that when we work for others, we are not only making the world a better place but we are healing ourselves. Those who extend themselves outward to humanity thrive on a higher level, are happier, healthier and live longer. Service work can release you from your cycle, get you out of the obsessive thought patterns regarding The Narcissist, and channel your heart center to worthy causes.

If we stay asleep or don't follow through with the 42 to 44 year old emotional maturity and the 51 year old spiritual awakening that Hand Clow speaks of, we will suffer even more into our 60s...unless we quickly and dramatically transform ourselves. I just went through my 42 to 44 transformational period: I gave up The Turks and trying to save men, quit public school teaching, entered into a Holistic Health Program with Massage Therapy, completed my yoga teaching certificate and re-created myself as a writer by starting my blog and writing here. I can be blissfully happy creating life on my own. This has been a period of great financial struggles as well. I buy nothing, need nothing and appreciate everything that I already have.

I have a strong and innate Will that emanates from my heart to help alleviate the suffering in the world. There are "underdogs" worth saving, however, you must learn to determine the difference between worthy underdogs and people that are destructive to your well being. For me, not helping someone, some creature in need, not giving everything that I have to stop suffering, is nearly impossible for my nature. I will always be an Open person, a healer, a feeler of the vibration of the universe, but I will be more awake in my surroundings, try to remove myself from my automatic response system formed by my childhood abuse, and act more consciously in everything I do.

EIGHT

THE EMPATHY LINK, PEOPLE-PLEASING & EMOTIONAL OBSESSIONS

According to everything we all read on blogs, facebook pages and even directly from Robert Hare's Psychopathy Checklist—Revised (PCL-R), Narcissists and Sociopaths lack Empathy and this factor is listed with the word "callous" next to it. Anyone that knows a lot, even a little, about Narcissism will mention the *lack of empathy*. I went against my intuition and mentioned this trait on my blog. I'm starting to wonder if we're all not just repeating without expanded vision.

Sociopaths and Narcissists have an Empathy Link (my term and concept) and it goes back to their childhood or when they experienced more innocent times; when they still operated from heart. In Turk Narc's case it is a positive Empathy Link and it goes back to feeling safe as a little boy receiving boundless love from his mother. Turk Narc spewed cruel words about heavy people we passed but he cringed at the thought of an older Turkish woman being poor, without food, and living in harsh conditions. His entire countenance dropped when we passed a thin, hunched over, elderly Turkish woman on a bridge in Istanbul selling chintzy tee-shirts to tourists. Though Turk Narc is not generous, he bought me a tee-shirt; a rare and spontaneous gift. With his face still drooped and forlorn, he expressed how much these images bothered him. Turk Narc feels empathy when a link is made to someone or something in his life that he feels bonded to and in his case, the emotional link goes to his elderly Turkish mother. The Turk Narc's mother is enabling and never set boundaries of control upon him when he was young...he considers her his *best friend*. His Empathy Link is to her and the fear that resides in his heart that she could have been born into similar circumstances.

My Sociopath's Empathy Link is of sadness and it goes back to when he still felt the suffering of the world around him and was powerless to do anything. His heart aches at the sight of hungry or injured animals. My Sociopath's child heart, mind, and emotions were tormented by the sounds of the screaming sheep and goats being slaughtered on the Muslim holiday, *Festival of Sacrifice*. He told me tales of the neglected animals of Turkey that were run over and left to die on the streets of his youth. Impressions of suffering and death can bruise the essence of any heart and mind, and later, when there is an echo of this in our environment, we flinch. He also enters a depressive state over animals starving because he often went hungry as a child when his father gave the food to his sister in front of his starving eyes; he watched her gulp food as hunger pangs ravished his insides. The cruelness of others create injured souls.

My Sociopath's empathy toward hungry or injured animals is counter to his hatred toward my dogs. My dogs represent ANOTHER love for me or my OTHER attention-giving source. Narcissists want your entire being and focus on them...they feel slighted and abandoned, as if they lost power and control when their current target has other loves or admirations in her life. The starving animals are not a threat to him; my dogs were. Also, he has no Empathy Link to well cared for and loved dogs because he grew up in harsh conditions. However, if one of my dogs were to become sick or injured, he would show a great amount of care and actually be sad; he would have control over my dogs and I would be in a weakened emotional condition. I've seen his sorrow when we were dealing with dying animals on the streets of Turkey and even when my cat died.

My Sociopath has an Empathy Link going back to not only being hungry but being cold during the brutally cold winters of Istanbul. His empathy activates with any sign of human body discomfort. His Empathy Link activated toward me during The Devalue stage and right before the final discard. If I were cold, he would madly run with concern in his face trying to cover me with blankets and he continually bought me new coats. He told me horror stories about his treatment at the hands of his Turkish father and then after decades of not talking to his father, he dropped everything in the US to return to Turkey to take care of him. He went into a tirade when he found his father in a urine soaked bed and scared every worker in the hospital into taking expert care of his former enemy from that point on. My Sociopath had to have overly washed and perfumed sheets every night as he grimaced and repeated tales of the condition he found his dying father in.

Narcissists recoil in seeing suffering because they know they could easily fall into the same position. Mr.Oh buys newspapers that he does not want from men who sell them at busy intersections. These men are part of a local drug and/or alcohol rehab program and are dealing with homelessness and living in shelters. He feels sorry for these men and shared with me that his greatest fear is being homeless.

Narcissists have no strong internal foundation and they exist feeling unstable...on a threshold. Seeing people in weakened conditions activates their sense of falling in.

The Narcissist & People-Pleasing & Emotional Obsessions

Narcissists are driven by Emotional Obsessions to people-please. The same emotionally obsessive drive that fuels their protecting underdogs. He emotionally obsessed over and people-pleased us into the wild, manic feelings in the beginning too. However, when real life entered into our relationship, or he had to be accountable, we became a less stimulating source of "love" and he turned to emotionally obsessing elsewhere. Intimate partners (after the chase) and close family members are considered simple, inferior and defective sources of attention and devotion because there is responsibility linked to them and there is no energy in this. In order to regain his energy, he hunts for more elusive and unknown sources to emotionally obsess over and to people-please; there is no weight of responsibility in this. His emotional obsessions are driven by his need to be loved and accepted without attached accountability.

He is a compulsive human-object-jumper filling his emotional cravings for quick acceptance by others. He amasses humans like some people amass fortunes. There is no quicker way to gain acceptance than through people-pleasing gestures such as picking up tabs and the doing of excessive favors. This keeps people around him at all times.

I relish in a man emotionally obsessing over me and taking great care of me in the honeymoon period. I become submissive, believing in my future life of being safe and cared for, and as a result, I allow him to control me. Then comes the transformation: his taking care of me into that of him violating all standards of trust and loyalty within our relationship. I grow weary, then too late in coming, assert myself to the shock and dismay of the man who craves to be needed without accountability.

The honeymoon period is of masks...both sides.

Narcissists glamorize images of people. There is no real-life involvement in unknown people and this sends him into an emotional place of exhilarating fun times with abundant smiles and lustful moments. Also, lesser known people have boundaries still erected and this makes them more interesting in a fantasy sort of way. Narcissists live in a constant state of *the grass is greener on the other side* and over *there*, he believes that he will find his sanctuary.

Narcissists live in a constant state of the grass is greener on the other side and over there, he believes, he will find his sanctuary.

He finds safety in the unfamiliar. He is emotionally charged up by the unfamiliar and emotionally dulled by the familiar. The emotionally familiar expects real emotional attachment and honesty from him and he is unable to give this. A Narcissist will assert himself viciously when he feels disrespected by an intimate partner, a former target or a family member but will succumb to real aggression and violations from strangers. Strangers are held more sacred than family. A Narcissist is delusional, paranoid and out of reality and believes that those closest to him are sources of danger, or rejection, and outsiders are safe people looking out for him.

The unfamiliar holds possibilities. This unfamiliar person (or object) will bring him elation until the end of time (narcissists have unrealistic and magical thinking)...while the familiar has already been ruined...ruined by him...therefore, discarded. You will find that people with personality disorders track down high-school crushes on the internet and live in a fantasy-world that if they meet up with this person, life will return to 16 year old first love and every day will be filled with wild and lustful romance. There is no consideration of the passage of time, or that the person now has a lot of baggage, or of the trials and responsibilities of adult life.

Narcissists people-please to keep a network of support around themselves or a safety-net of security because they have no foundation of self; they have no solid inner-core or sense of being in which they can draw upon to feel grounded and spirit-infused. They have no inner-dwelling place in which to go to in order to draw inspiration, insight or self-motivation. They live completely through outer sources of attention and stimulation, from people and objects. Thus, people and objects are the same in their eyes. This outside energy prevents him from ever having to go inside himself or having to access his own light from his own soul. He does not have endorsement of his soul; his soul influence is turned off. His soul light is replaced by outside sources instead of inside motivations.

Narcissists have no Will to evolve. He only has energy and motivation toward seeking people stimulation. WILL is an innate vision on what needs to be done and the clear insight toward the illuminated goals that are laid out on one's path. Winning people over through superficial people-pleasing stimulates him, whereas working on creating a greater life, stronger relationships and a healthier-self bores him. Independent work is needed to improve as a human being and this requires delayed gratification, whereas people-pleasing is instant gratification. Narcissists have no ability for delayed gratification. He would rather people-please for his needed life energy (receiving adoration from others) instead of working toward higher achievements.

People-pleasing is simple, superficial, and transitory; it is instant gratification involving instant smiles and instant adoration. Building a healthy relationship takes time, loyalty and steadfastness and delayed gratification is required. Narcissists seek instant gratification because of their addictive personality that needs constant stimulation.

(WILL is different from Willpower. Willpower is forced energy toward something that is not an innately strong and pulling force and therefore, the goals are not clear and great effort is needed to go in that direction.)

The Inappropriate Relationship Boundaries of A Narcissist

The Adult Child

My Sociopath Post: 3.11.15

Narcissists never have healthy intimate relationships with healthy partners because they habitually lie to cover up their life of Emotionally Obsessing over inappropriate sources. Once the wild and erratic honeymoon period is over with the most recent intimate partner, he seeks ego stimulation from most any other source. He turns salespeople into his "good friends" when it was only a business transaction, a recent past lover into "she's like a sister" when they barely got along previously, and his adult children into pseudo 'boyfriends and girlfriends.' A Narcissist has no boundaries and moderation within relationships: He is either putting all his energies into intensely charming a new target into loving him, thereby neglecting everyone and everything else around him, or he is putting the recently won-over new target on the shelf to obsessively seek the adoration of others.

This lack of moderation is particularly true with his adult children. His children grow to hate him because of his cold, emotional-detachment toward them and their mother and how easily he discarded them and moved on to make another family. However, as these children grow into adults, their feelings toward him fluctuate between wanting him in their life and avoiding him. At the point of their wanting him, The Narcissist pulls his adult children back into a relationship with him but it will not be with appropriate boundaries and controls. He does not behave as a good and strong father-figure that guides them into being healthy and strong adults, but instead he tries to be their best friend and even attempts to turn them into "boyfriends" or "girlfriends." He acts as their "boy toy" and enabler for their laziness and bad life decisions. He only cares about them insofar as winning their approval and being stimulated by their favorable response to his "boy toy" act.

He lacks generational boundaries. He does not emotionally bond with his children...he Emotionally Obsesses for their approval.

Since The Narcissist can NEVER be alone, he uses his children as a form of entertainment. In the case of an adult-daughter that recently hated him and is now in hate-remission, he turns her into his newest "girlfriend" and whereas she recently had no contact with him, he sets up a situation where he obsessively dotes over her to win her approval. He lavishes money on the daughter thereby neglecting the needs of the intimate partner, and he is unavailable to his partner because of the inappropriate time and energy spent with the daughter.

Narcissists are susceptible to exploitation because of their obsessive and desperate need for approval. It is likely the adult-daughter has her own personality-issues because of having had an emotionally-detached narcissistic father, and she realizes the father is now trying to be her "boyfriend," so she takes advantage of this and exploits his attention and extreme generosity. She uses and manipulates him too. Eventually this blows up in his face. Just like with everything in his life, he becomes easily bored with his pseudo, intimate partner and moves on to obsess elsewhere and as a result, the daughter goes into a tirade.

Though the adult-child was used as an example, The Narcissist creates this same dynamic with everyone, including us: Emotionally Obsess (we mistake this for love and emotional connection), Detach, Emotionally Obsess elsewhere. The primary intimate partner is the one that suffers the most because of his lies and delusions regarding his compulsive need for adoration from inappropriate sources and his lack of boundaries and moderation in his relationships. END POST

Narcissists people-please salespeople. He is loyal to insignificant strangers. People that are not yet smitten by and under-the-control of The Narcissist are interesting in an 'off-limits sort of way;' they stand out of and away from his control so he reveres and glamorizes them. He can't say "no" to their contracts and commitments because he is intimidated and is afraid to appear mean, bad, or cheap; he puts his family at financial risk. He thinks he is special in the eyes of salespeople, that he is really liked, and this excites him and he deludes himself that he has a new, great friend that will look out for him; he is only being sold a sales-pitch. You will hear a Narcissist refer to a person he does business with as his "good friend." He is often exploited by people who overcharge him and lure him into bad contracts.

A Narcissist does not intelligently think through transactions; he merely seeks the energy from the approval he gains by making the salesperson happy.

A Narcissist will over-tip waitresses, even for bad service, because he wants to please and impress her...even though he may never see her again. Also, he believes the waitress is smitten by him when she is only doing her job, therefore, he falls in lust or goes into a state of emotional obsession. He believes she is giving him special service: greater food quality and bigger portions. There is yet another psychological side to this: The Underdog Element. Male Narcissists (heterosexual) see female waitresses as underdogs and therefore alluring. Underdog = Submission & Loyalty. This is why, too, The Narcissist believes prostitutes and porn women are "amazing quality" and are only doing these low-level jobs for the extra side-money she needs for some altruistic life that she is living; and when she has sex with him, she will fall in love with him and they will run off together to live an amazing life. (This also relates to the Narcissist's fixation on superficial image and to take this further...The Narcissistic male fantasy that Vietnamese, Thai, Russian, Ukrainian, etc., women will bring him a life of submission and compliance and therefore, elation, satiation and happiness, when many of these women have been trained from childhood to use an American man for money, security and US Citizenship.)

Salespeople, service workers, or other street smart and savvy individuals intuitively detect that they are dealing with an insecure people-pleaser and they will give him inferior products and overcharge him; they know that he will not complain or check his bill for accuracy. The Narcissist's submission to service workers also emanates from his innate fear and inferiority complex that others are naturally stronger than he is; he intuitively knows that he has no identity, no self, and that others do (yes, even prostitutes can have a strong sense-of-self).

The Empath & People-Pleasing

Empaths are driven by a higher spirit. We operate heart-center and see all animals and humans as our brothers and sisters on the evolutionary path and hold responsibility for their safe-keeping. We can intuitively see, hear, and feel the pain in the world and of the planet. Empaths people-please because we not only care deeply about everything and everyone, but we can't stand to hurt the feelings of others, and will instead put our own well-being at risk. We walk in Harmlessness. However, we do have emotional breakdowns that result in our *thrashing about* when our compassion and forgiving nature is repeatedly violated.

Empaths live in accordance with the Universal Law of Redemption and seek to prove that goodness dominates and will prevail. We work on a higher soul and spiritual plane and are more attuned to the advanced Aquarian Age than those humans who are still operating instinctually from the animal gut. We people-please from a sense of spreading good vibrations. In a sense, we are pushing human evolution despite its pushing back. This is opposed to why The Narcissist people-pleases: to gain instant attention, recognition, glamour, support and ego-supply.

I was about 10-years-old when I walked into the dark woods in my backyard to feed the wild animals. With bread in my hands that I carefully tore in perfect bite-size pieces, I put my offerings out to the first wondering raccoon that I spotted. He (she?) walked up to my hand, looked at its contents, and bit me. I ran in terror more from hurt feelings than from the pain of my injury. I was afraid to tell my parents what happened and cried while washing and caring for my own hand because the attempted wild animal feeding was a failure.

I learned as a young girl to be quiet. Any sounds would set my mother into a rage. These sounds could be my brothers and me playing joyfully, or our coming to mother to tell her that a neighborhood bully hurt us, or even that we needed something. In the case of a mean neighborhood kid, I was barked at for being the one that did something bad to deserve the meanness. Unlike today's children, where their needs are constantly met, my brothers and I were not allowed to ask for anything including a drink if we were thirsty from playing outside. Our household was on a strict eating and drinking schedule: Breakfast, Lunch, Dinner. Drinking was only permitted after a meal, not during; we had three beverages a day and nothing in between. I was trained to never ask for anything and that my needs were selfish and if I should ever go to my mother, there would be an emotional explosion: I didn't want her to commit suicide. I knew from a young age that if she did, it would be my fault.

If only I were this strict about my relationship decisions! I only become strict when dealing with the aftermath of harm and then it is too late. I've lost all power and am reactionary. Now, my response to harm comes in the form of reading and writing on abuse and publicly advocating to spread awareness. Writing is the output of my stress response system. Everyone needs to have some type of Form Building (manifesting something outside self) for their internal energies.

You will hear a Narcissist proudly exclaim that he wants a "low maintenance" partner. He will glow when he says this because he believes this is what he deserves; it is his right. This proud statement also comes from arrogance: *I am great and I deserve another "great" person, aka., low-maintenance. I shouldn't have to expend any energy or effort to have someone in my life; people, especially women that I have sex with, will be in my life merely because it is a privilege* (he believes his penis and his *manly* hormones to be the key to the universe). In The Narcissist's twisted world, he not only wants a compliant sex-partner and female entertainer, but he wants a woman that doesn't ask for much and is a caretaker and a mother-figure. He spends his life pursuing honeymoon idolization and yet screaming and grabbing for mother.

Codependents live through a brainwashing program that was instilled within us by our Narcissistic Parent(s), that manifest into attracting and mating with Narcissistic partners, to our ingrained thought-pattern that "low maintenance" is a great quality. We want and desire to make The Narcissist happy because in our people-pleasing nature, we believe he deserves a great and non-demanding person because he is *superior* and by not asking for anything, and by being easy-going, we have succeeded in making this great person happy: We are his perfect match. *Those other demanding women are selfish and I am good, pure, unconditional loving, and I have achieved the greatest reward of all time: A tough, in control, intense, sexy, charismatic, charming, alluring, manly, powerful, elusive and the most desirable man on earth....A Narcissist.*

It's easy to understand why a Narcissist wants a people-pleaser: He gets all his needs and desires fulfilled without his expansion of energy and she easily places her needs, health, happiness and life second. The Narcissist has a built in radar that navigates to entwine himself in the life of a codependent, pleasing, selfless, workhorse, excessively loyal, trustworthy and committed partner. He will not work hard in a relationship (past the winning-over stage); he is lazy, disorganized, irresponsible, shallow, and cheap (once the target is won over).

Many Empath people-pleasers never experienced unconditional love and acceptance so we are programmed to act in a way where we never receive anything easily, especially love. Narcissists are the perfect challenge for us: Give everything and fight to receive little in return. We are the people that accept crumbs. Basically, we live a life through a deep programming that echos undeserving even though we are the hardworking, dedicated, loyal, smart and accomplished: The personality disordered brainwashed us from a young age to not only feel inferior but to take a secondary position. He is able to accomplish this because he walks, talks, and acts with an inflated sense of superiority and importance whereas we doubt, downplay and deflate our strengths.

My physical appearance had to be a people-pleasing image out into the world as a reflection of my parents' status (they couldn't care less about causing my inner-madness). I got contacts when I was 12 and every time I lost or broke one I froze in fear for the wrath that would result. I broke a hard contact and put the two-halves back in my eye swearing to my mother that it shattered when I blinked. My mother called the eye doctor and demanded an emergency appointment. I stood in the office with fear-placed eye-shards as the doctor stood shaking his knowing head. I got braces at 13 when I didn't really need them; my bite was perfect. I had a small space in the front of my two front teeth and it had to be fixed. Later, Carly Simon made the space between the two front teeth her sexy and unique feature. My mother always reflected on the image of Carly and told me when I was older, "Maybe we should have let you keep that space in your teeth."

I had to be my mother's silent, robotic, unemotional, unfeeling, unbeing clone that was to exist only as an image on tiptoe. My "tiptoe" was also on a literal level. My father hated sounds except for his own screams. This meant when I walked down the narrow hallway of our 1960s ranch home and I entered into the kitchen area, I was not to be heard. My father always sat in the family room that was at the opposite end of the house from the bedrooms and one step beneath the kitchen. He sat staring at the TV against the farthest wall of our long home. As I approached the kitchen from my bedroom, I was not to scrape my slippers or drag my bare feet. My ankles crackled as I walked during my growth spurt: I learned to roll my feet...heel to ball. This no-sound applied to eating as well. I was not allowed to make any sounds with fork, spoon or knife against my plate...that *clink* sound. I was the one designated to wash dishes after a meal and I was not permitted to make any noises while rinsing the plates and silverware; nothing was allowed to come in contact with anything else. Even the cupboards were not allowed to make a *click* when opening or closing; I learned to roll the cupboards just like my feet.

Narcissists want someone that is seen and not heard. I was a Great Soundless Person for The Narcissists in my life. As a child, I survived by being quiet and never asking for anything. As an adult, I tried to survive by bending toward the whims of others. We are to be their reflection and NOT a separate human entity with wants, needs, and desires. We are to feed their ego and external needs and to not have a healthy ego of our own. We are to be in awe of him and his grandiosity and this comes by constantly complimenting him (Empaths are genuine payers of compliments to make others feel good) and placing his needs first: I was a vegan for many years while with Turk Narc when veganism wasn't well known. When dining out, my options were extremely limited. I would order an inexpensive side dish, not wanting to cost him money and that was vegan qualified, and would quietly sit and watch Turk Narc eat off my small plate. I could not share from his plate filled with meat and dairy. I felt as if I didn't have a right to my small portion of food and wanting this to myself meant that I was selfish.

Empaths need to put themselves, their goals and needs first. We can then better serve humanity. If there is a good person in our life, then he/she will understand that our needs are priority and try to compliment and help us. We, in turn, can safely offer our support and help others toward their goals and aspirations. But because we can be blind people-pleasers that operate from low self-esteem, we must first wait before we go into action for another person's needs. We need to take relationships slowly so that we can analyze our surroundings, or use our mental faculties to override our heart-led emotionalism, to better ensure our safety. There will be some people that we can form a team with based upon equality and there will be others that throw us back into secondary position. Be deliberate, not wayward.

NINE

SIBLINGS OF ABUSE

Siblings that come from abusive, neglectful or dysfunctional homes often have estranged relationships with each other later in life. One would think it would be the opposite; that a closeness of ties would be forever strong and durable and we would be soul connecting confidants; after all, no one went through the same circumstances of your childhood as you and your sibling(s).

In actuality, the siblings from the same chaotic homes often ride on their own planet of despair, dealing with trauma in their own private and guarded way. There is a razor sharp division of the traumatized spirits of these siblings and a separation of inner processing. Whereas one sibling recognizes the abuse, the other sibling denies it. Even with regard to the sibling that registers the abuse, it may be on a confused, surface-level only and he/she may not know how to bring it to a full and clear vision. The pain and shame involved in our processing of trauma is hidden away, even to our sibling(s). For each sibling has different processing abilities and one (or more) may even stay trapped under the brainwashing powers of the caretaker(s), or in the belief that "things didn't really happen," or "things weren't that bad."

Both my brothers are alcoholics. I should be one too, or perhaps a drug-addict or street prostitute, but I became addicted to learning instead; there is no end to learning so it keeps me busy. I say "street prostitute" because it would take self-esteem to be a "high-priced" escort. Both brothers say something and immediately take it back out of fear of not only our mother, but of having to face the realness of their damaged souls. My older brother is a good-natured alcoholic that gives all his money away to make friends. My younger brother is bitter, harsh and unforgiving toward family members, even those that try to be kind toward him. He contradicts everything said by everyone...even himself. Younger brother has little to do with me except for sporadic drunken phone calls because I am the only one of the family that has ever dared to use the "abuse" word (though the last time I attempted to use this word with him was over twenty years ago and he went into a violent rage fit against me). I never had an angry or confrontational word with either brother; we are mere strangers that fear the shame that is revealed in each other's eyes. Siblings carry the shame and burden of their parents' mental and emotional dysfunction into their relationships with each other.

My mother guilted us into fear and shame if we dare talked about anything from our past. If I ever tried to approach anything to do with my childhood, except for the quick burst of "fun" that my father spun us all in for a short period-of-time, she would turn into a spiraling vortex of destruction. Her outburst would resemble the grayish-greenish face of The Exorcist girl; head turning backwards with green protruding vomit. My mother literally squeezed her face into a contorted configuration, hissed and spit, when someone said something she didn't agree with. She would then scream at me that I was engaging in "stupid psycho-babble talk" and that I was like my aunts (father's sisters) whom my father and her called "nuts." Mothers who have no control over their emotions create basket-case children.

Just recently, older brother calls me and cries without crying but more begging from a raw soul that's been gutted,"she (mother) used to say she wished I were dead." My mouth hung open. She said that to him too? I calmly tell him that *SHE was just as much part of it as HE was (father) and he needs to stop allowing her to brainwash him.* My older brother never moved out of our small town and lives in one of my mother's properties...an old farmhouse made into an antique store that my mother opened for one-month and then gave up on it because a customer asked her what the price was for an unmarked doll. My mother told this customer and when the woman asked if she would accept less, my mother exclaimed, "Take it for one penny then." The woman did just that and immediately after, my mother closed the store forever. My brother now lives in bric-a-brac; he sleeps on a relic bed and stores his food in a vintage refrigerator.

I attempt to shed light in his heart that bleeds and say: *She tells us everyone is crazy, no one has a happy family, everyone hates each other.* My brother's mental processing whips around in an instant and he bites his own tail saying, **Get over it! Some people had it worse, at least we weren't raped, I'm over it, I'm happy, Why can't you be?** He did a complete reversal in a two-sentence conversation. You will see this "word salad" or "circle-talk-hell" with adults who were abused and brainwashed as children (and those with personality disorders). I know this is a screaming and confused soul and I try to process it as such without reacting outwardly toward him.

Older brother tried to emerge into light and then retreated back into his little-boy-self under the power of a mentally-ill mother...he knows, he's trained to submit like a broken-spirited dog, that if he says anything to her, to me, to anyone about his pain, that mother's damaged spirit is floating nearby and *she will know*...she will spew out terrifying sobs of, "I can't take the guilt...we had good times...I was trying to save your lives." (Mother convinced us that she had to stay with father because if she didn't, he would have murdered us). Older brother remains his fragmented self: a broken wall where its shattered pieces were haphazardly taped together by a sick mother's psyche so that a mere image of a man, her son, could stand upon this earth. This shadowy outline of a man tries to add his own mortar to his weakly constructed brick foundation of humanness but can only take this foreign feeling of strength for a moment and he abandons the effort...mother might punish him for building his own man-wall.

He then turns on me, runs to our mother and repeats some version of what I said to him when I was confirming and elaborating on his initial cry. My brother is now the sensible one that is on mother's good side and I am the *crazy* one of the family. My mother's screams would soon bellow out at me across the phone lines. She creates fear and shame between her children's interactions with one another. I now realize there cannot be interaction between us because my mother's sickness manifests and lingers nearby. Older brother is now leaving me voicemails with brief stand-up comedy routines impersonating either Dr. Phil or Maury requesting my appearance on their show to talk my "family abuse psychobabble." The broken souls are the ones that joke the most. Robin Williams committed suicide during the editing of this book.

My brother has severe and permanent brain damage from being a child of monsters and the self-medicating effects of drinking alcohol since 15-years-old to calm down his nervous system. Abused children become adults that don't feel in body; we feel ungrounded, unstable, floating, insecure in our humanness and our place in society and among people; we feel that we don't fit in with other humans. My brother does escape my mother for moments in time as in those phone calls to me. It was one of his many quick escapes out of Her but he ultimately cries for Her safety-net and retreats back inside Her and says something exactly as She says it. He may not feel internally at peace while repeating Her words like a parrot, but it serves as his homing instinct; he returns to Her.

The feeling of being ungrounded applies to narcissists and empaths or addicts. Narcissists and Empaths are on opposite ends of the spectrum but they can have similar lost feelings. The effects are opposite in manifestation: Narcissists are extremely self-centered and use and exploit others for their own gain, whereas Empaths are extremely selfless and give of themselves to the feeding of others to the point of their own detriment.

I wish that my brother could do many more of these erratic jumps from Her to eventually build strength and endurance to make the final and long lasting leap across the bridge to freedom but I know that won't happen. He is now 50-years-old and there would have to be more areas of struggles and studying one's self, no matter how slow going, to progress toward an awakening than what his brain is capable of. This leap into awareness is easier to come by with people that continue to pursue learning, education and more expanded experiences after high school and into their later years. These minds are more apt to be able to first recognize childhood brainwashing and to try to veer from the effects. My brother stopped learning and growing after high school. People that stop learning at a young age tend to have more limited capabilities and cannot form or grow new thought patterns. My brother will never break from my mother's torment; he will always be bound and tied by her strings.

A mother's soul infuses into her children. If this is a dangerous soul blending, we must recognize it and break free from it.

In order to heal and to ultimately grow, we must continually expand our physical brain, mental body and consciousness while controlling our emotional body; this takes effort. Developing Wisdom, or a higher level of thinking, knowing and realizing, is the key to our freedom. It is not enough to just know something...it must be applied...this takes forced effort.

When it comes to expansion of our minds, learning and overall consciousness, we must:

1. **Realize:** *(I attract unhealthy relationships and sacrifice my personal health and development as a result.)*

2. **Apply:** *(I will stay away from intimate relationships until I get healthy.)*

3. **Utilize:** *(I will take time to improve my life [home; finances; job], to become a better writer and creator, and to improve the overall workings of my mind through higher-level activities that involve*

learning and growing (taking classes; learning new things; reading/watching mind-evolving materials...)

My younger brother manifests more outward anger than my older brother. He hates (or perhaps fears) anything that connects to traumatic childhood memories, and though I never harmed him in any way, I am a connection to that trauma. He calls me while drunk and incessantly cusses just like my father. Not directly at me, but more in using cuss words as commas. His physical manifestation, or gruff language pattern, is that of my father but his emotional processing is that of my mother's: *Fuck, everyone hates their family, all families are fucken' crazy and we are the most normal. It's just drama when families get together on Thanksgiving, I'm glad each of us spent it alone, that's more normal, I hate drama. Don't you remember, shit, we had fun times with dad. We just think too fucken' much, don't fucken' think...we are all normal, everyone else is fucken' crazy.* These were all my mother's words: I heard these same words, without the cussing, going back to when I could remember.

This was all unprompted...I wasn't "thinking" and nor did I say anything about any type of family. I wasn't even speaking. My brother was having an emotional release of locked-up trauma energy in his nervous system that was the brainwashing of our mother: **No one should feel, speak of, or react to being destroyed in the family home. Get over IT and move on!** Her soul was resonating through the ether and he heard its echo.

High atop a mountain an echo calls out to direct the family below to look up and out of where they are trapped in the valley low...the echo only irritates their closed-off minds for they cannot hear any sound they're not familiar with.

My mother keeps all her children in her emotional prison. My siblings and I have a violent and emotionally trapped ghost of a mother that lingers in our breadth, and especially in the space that is supposed to contain natural sibling love. We are all afraid to speak to one another, and afraid to mention anything of a true nature to our mother; we are all locked away from words that can heal.

Younger brother was also doing circle-talk-hell as a result of being raised by a gaslighting mother. He was repeating my mother's words via her warped perception while still trying to break through her brainwashing without seeing the brainwashing that made him grow into the suffering adult that he is now. He had moments of clarity where he broke through and would say, "I want to go on mental disability, I think I should, but it's too hard to get approved." He was seeing his torment, trying to express it, but then he would quickly snap back into a stream of, "we think too much, other people are dumb and don't think...all parents are screwed up, there are so many factors, so many factors..." If I said anything at this time, I would throw my brother out of his emergence into clarity and logic and back into our mother's mind and I would be the enemy again. I remained quiet as he fought not only himself, but my mother.

My older brother is the Damaged-Innocent, he punishes himself...he is a gentle and crying drinker and though this band-aid habit is harmful, he does it to push down his haunts. My younger brother is the Damaged-Angry...he is hurt but the result is hurting others through drinking and angry speech. However, I am certain that both are not sociopaths.

Emotional chaos needs to be moved into the intellect or mental where it can be hashed out and then a new emotional sense formed from an impersonal level. A beginning step is to not take abuse personally. Abuse is not about the personal You. You could be anyone and the abuser will still abuse.

My brothers and I remain single and living alone. Odd, all three siblings in one small family. Narcissists endlessly cycle through relationships and their collateral damage stop having relationships...hiding away from pain. I'm trying to heal so independence is good for me but my brothers suffer and drown in denial.

A Narcissist Sibling In The Mix

When a Narcissist or Sociopath evolves out of one of these siblings, the dynamics are different. The sibling of a Narcissist has learned from a young age the crazy-making that this disordered sibling can cause in the family unit. Narcissistic traits develop at a young age and the sibling may be the first to notice this: being blamed for things The Narcissist did; having toys/belongings taken, destroyed and/or mishandled by The Narcissist; witnessing the young Narcissist learning to lie, manipulate, and get away with it. The non-narcissist sibling either attempts to fight it out with The Narcissist and ultimately gets squashed, or learns to enable the bad sibling for easier survival.

A symbiotic relationship will likely evolve into Adult Narcissist Sibling and Adult Enabling Sibling. Both halves will present themselves to the world as loving and close. However, the Narcissist half of the pair, has a harder time doing this, and actually resents his enabling sibling, and will act lovingly only when he needs the sibling's support for trouble he gets himself into, i.e., legal matters or when he is devaluing or discarding a partner. It is very common for the enabling sibling to make false statements and to act as a false witness in court during the many legal suits/divorces/child-custody conflicts The Narcissist is always entwined in.

In some cases, both siblings turn out to be Narcissists or Sociopaths. This could be evil supporting and working alongside evil, or, evil hating evil but making great co-supporters.

The sibling of My Sociopath was a harmful enabler and backed up My Sociopath's twisted and chaotic life of shattered lives and his continuing tumultuous events. Of course, she supported him in his always being a "victim" role. I believe she walked with closed eyes, was not very smart (not all educated people are smart), and therefore, danced blindly with My Sociopath as he played out the role of her perpetually victimized, younger brother. However, in this sickly entwined Sociopath/Sibling relationship there was an added cultural shadow of conditioning. In Turkey, girl children are placed inferior to boy children. This sister was not only Sociopath trained to be enabling but to be in second position to him.

It is uncanny how Sociopathy spreads as slippery deceit into the personalities of other family members and even down into the next generation. This enabling and dangerous sister was a Psychologist. She was not a natural healer but she was street smart. She knew that if she got an online degree in the United States she could take the title of US Doctor to Turkey and would be glamorized by the Turks as having superior American credentials. The Turks understand little beyond the title, "American Doctor." However, she barely passed classes in the subpar, online PhD program and was banned from taking the state exams. She had to petition a different state for permission to take their exams.

I got tripped up by the workings of these two siblings, their interplay between each other and the deceptive imagery that they cast around those that enter the scene. I was initially fooled by her degree and title and therefore, went to her about concerns that I had with My Sociopath, and at this time, I was a mangled mess on how to not only interpret what I was going through, but how to express *IT* to this Sister Psychologist. She convinced me that this very rocky road with My Sociopath was a normal part of relationships and I should be patient. I allowed my own thoughts to wither away, doubted my own intuition and fell into the enabling sister's trap. I stayed much longer with My Sociopath when a secure-in-thought and intuitively grounded person would have fled.

Polarity, or opposition, occurs between siblings from dysfunctional homes. Polarity shows in two ways:

- ◆ Confusion about the mental versus emotional processing of the events that happened.

- ◆ Bitterness that one sibling projects toward another sibling that sees the abuse and dysfunction.

You will see a rift in sibling relationships. In many cases, the female sibling sees the abuse more clearly as it is typical for females to be more emotionally aware of their past surroundings and how it relates to their current life; they can mentally access this easier. Male siblings are more emotionally bonded and blindly devoted to the *Pure and Loving Mother Essence* delusion.

In contrast, there could be a cohesiveness between two damaged siblings where one enables and supports the more harmful one. You will notice the more enabling one is overly accepting and indulgent of the disordered one and continually shows up to defend him in his many bad life events.

TEN

TRAPPED IN MOTHER'S EMOTIONAL BODY

The Sexual Aspect

A child takes on the emotional condition of their mother. The mother is where our first intimate and emotional bond occurs. Our father is not of an intimate, emotional connection, but more of a physical and mental. A child may instead take on the father's physical mannerisms, traits and habits regarding life such as motivation level, work skills and habits and social position. We think about and process our relationship to our fathers more on an intellectual brain level (for those who do try to process their childhood). I can mentally process that my father was psychologically ill but when I inwardly cringe for my shattered life, I emotionally think of my mother's role, or mostly her vacancy, her void, her inability to love and bond with her children...the fact that she sacrificed her children for another damaged soul. I am more removed from my father's monsters and instead emotionally linked to my mother's. A mother who emotionally bonds with her child can remove the child from an abusive environment, even though she may believe it to be too late, with a great chance that the child will recover. However, my mother kept us all trapped in an abyss because her mind was in a cage of martyrdom and powerlessness.

Children most often stay trapped in the mother's emotional body, or psyche, for the duration of their life and then pass this emotional condition onto their own children. The mother's emotional body is: degree of joy and positivity; ability to think logically; level and quality of problem-solving skills; manner in which a crisis is dealt with; spiritual and/or God attitudes and beliefs; quality (not quantity) of social relationships; ideas about and contributions to the world outside herself; treatment and response to her children and how she teaches them to respond to her; and the overall quality of family that she creates, strives to improve upon, and tries to protect.

My mother believes anything that she thinks or feels, or does not think or feel, is true for all humans. Just like a Narcissist, she believes herself to be omniscient. Since she hated her children and my father (it was a love/hate feeling with him) she believed all mothers hated their children and all wives hated their husbands; she took her own thoughts, feelings, emotions and applied them on a general basis to everyone. She then transmitted her mind-created ideology to her children, in particular, to me. This is similar to the mind-isolating thinking pattern of someone with autism. My mother does not have conversations with her children...she says a few words regarding hate for humanity and if we veer from saying similar, she screams that she wishes we were dead and threatens to commit suicide.

This affects me to this day...I am extremely careful with and neurotic about my speech. I find myself feeling bad when I try to stand up for myself when someone does a blatant wrong to me. **The other person who inflicted the overt harm, stands in calm, quiet reserve, or Narcissistic Control, as I squirm to try to protect myself from the wrong that I think I am.** Narcissists and Sociopaths cannot be around people who are assertive, aggressive, verbally crass or careless, rude or overpowering, or who may inadvertently insult them. The gentle souls that are careful with their words and speak with deliberate and controlled kindness toward others are those that are swallowed up by aggressors and bullies.

Since our mothers are our first and only reference point of life and bonding, their emotional legacy becomes our own. I was a little girl about 7-years-old and like all children, I craved my parents' love but didn't understand that they weren't giving it. I quietly burrowed into my parents' bed one night with a big, red, stuffed fox. It was almost as big as me and came from one of our local town carnivals. I wish I could blame it on an Ohio thunder and lightning storm and that I was scared but this wasn't the case. What compelled me to slide into my parents' bed with that fox is inconceivable: I knew at seven that it was wrong to assert myself for love and it was especially pushy to add a fox to this desperate attempt; but the fox made me appear more childlike, so in a way, it was savvy thinking. I pretended to be asleep, snuggling the big fox in an attempt to create a scene that I was a small bird in a protective nest. I heard my mother hissing outside the room to my father, *Get HER out of there!* My mother was incapable of dealing with a small girl, with a fox, lying in her bed, pretending to be asleep. I was young and I was still a bit brave in seeking out love. As an adult, I still seek love in the scary while emotionally holding a big, stuffed fox for protection. I don't know what happened to that fox but I wish I still had it so that it could sit on that rocking chair.

My Sociopath told me that as a very young boy during a cold, Istanbul winter, he slept with his mother to keep warm. His father came home very late after womanizing and proceeded to have sex with his mother as My Younger Sociopath lie frozen (both physically and emotionally) in bed against her. He vividly described to me, with sickness in his face, the sex sounds his parents made fifty years ago and 10,000 miles away...in what was supposed to be a warm bed with emotionally safe parents. This terminated any chance of him developing his own healthy emotional body, in particular with regard to having intimate, loving, trusting, and bonding relationships with women. Hearing his mother's and father's sex screams, actually being so close that he absorbed the vibrations, traumatized and halted any chance of My Sociopath developing and being healthily grounded in areas of true intimacy.

The first memory of his mother was that she was a screamer, a grunter, someone pounced on by a menacing and dark figure that he feared...a mother that failed to provide her little boy, lying next to her, comfort and security...instead, she removed herself from the little boy's emotional security and gave away all her control to a bad man. The bad man and his low-level needs came first; the little boy didn't come at all. She satiated the devil's desires over any chance that her child may develop into an integrated soul or whole human being. I do understand that this was not only the 1950s but it was 1950's Turkey and women did not have the opportunities as they do now, but the effects of the bad man on the child is the same, and free women in free nations still choose bad men to be the fathers of their children. Mothers that are emotionally absorbed by and give their essence or soul over to bad men, create children that grow into adults that are fragmented on all levels: mental (developmental and learning disabilities); emotional (psychological and personality disorders); physical (health issues); and sexual (porn and other unhealthy sex addictions or hangups).

Sociopaths not only conquer a target's current sexual life, but her past and future intimate life. Any of her past, or potential, sexual encounters are a threat to his conquering and controlling sperm. Soon after the honeymoon period, he punishes her for her sexual past and any sexual male-figure in her surroundings. Her past punishable intimate encounters can include her long-term committed relationships or even a marriage. He mentally whips the woman for having sexual needs and for ever fulfilling these needs and his out-lash even comes as a result of her having sex with him. He erupts with insecurity because he cannot bond on a deep and sexual level...he is a mere shell that primitively and instinctively seeks sex to conquer and subjugate his prey. He is horny and knows in his primitive brain-stem that when he penetrates a woman, she falls under the control of his mental and emotional trappings.

Most women are instinctively driven to bond on an emotional and mental level with men they are sexually intimate with. The woman emotionally entwines with the man she is having sex with for survival of her babies and for the making of a secure family-unit. He will ultimately push her away because not only is she a human creature with emotions, but she can express herself deeply through sexual intimacy...he cannot. He only appears to be making love during his wild and ego-driven honeymoon period or when the fresh target is adoring him. In actuality, this *love making* is him making love to himself in response to your being enamored with him and his body. A sexually, and sensually, loving woman threatens him and he hates this aspect of her soon after he conquers her emotions.

My Sociopath is emotionally obsessed with sex but has no ability to express sexuality in a solid and grounded way. He stands on a high and commanding platform when he explains that he will never return to a woman after The Discard....that *she is dirty, soiled*...even if she claims to have not been with another man during their separation; he believes that since she may have even thought about another man, she is tainted. He applies a contradictory version of this thinking to himself: During the final stage of The Discard with me, and upon one of his many returns to me, he cried in a wail of an injured animal voice, "But, I'm *clean*. I kept myself *clean*." He was referring to the fact that he didn't have sex with anyone else...though he tried and was rejected. He was preying upon many other target sources, but they all let him down in someway, so he made a last ditch effort to regain my adoration to redeem his rejected ego.

My Sociopath does not use The Discard in his language, but he proudly proclaims that he can *immediately and completely forget a woman once she slights him in any way*...that he can *shut her off*. When he told me this I confused him for a strong man determined in his beliefs.

He bragged to me that he did The Discard when he was 14-years-old. My Sociopath had a flirting ritual with a young girl: She rode her bike back and forth in front of his house and underneath the window where he stood; he did the same past her house and under the window where she stood. This lasted for months...one day, the girl failed to do the ritual. He immediately, within an instant, lost all feelings for her...his *first love*. The girl could have been sick, her family could have gone away for the weekend...it didn't matter, she slighted him and was now The Discarded...she failed to spark him alive that one day as he stood in front of that window waiting for her attention; he took this as rejection. We will never be safe with someone who has a personality disorder; they are never loyal. They will run, in an instant, to the quickest and shallowest source of attention and validation.

My Sociopath's immediate emotional discard applies if his woman makes a nice comment about another man. He is now the disrespected and rejected man...all her energy is not onto him but a splatter of it went elsewhere: Sociopath Rejection. My Sociopath said that a man in our social circle could not get a woman. I casually responded that he had a lot going for him: looks, personality, intelligence, a good job, a nice home. Looking back now, My Sociopath discarded me at this moment. There was NO going back to his pedestaling me because I *admired* another. Whereas he was previously kept alive by a full shower of my admiration sparks, I inadvertently let one of these sparks fly off toward another direction. I was ruined and tainted...*dirty*. Sociopaths discard us in a flash of time because of a flash of our humanness. My Sociopath immediately triangulated this man and me; he used words to orchestrate negative feelings: My Sociopath transmitted to me, "Sam hates animals," and to Sam, "She abuses me."

Turk Narc is detached from real intimacy in sexual relationships and does not care who is having sex with whom. This not only applies to himself but his current sexual partner. His mother doted on him yet was cold and rigid toward everyone else. Sex is of a Hedonistic nature to him and for gratification and release only. If his *committed* partner has sex with someone else he confidently feels secure in his grandiosity that he is superior to the other man so it was her step down. He is self-assured that he is the greatest lover, the most amazing specimen of manhood ever, and that she will want him more in the end anyway. This is how a Narcissist brainwashes his partners: *You will never find anyone better than me.* Turk Narc is cold and separated from deep intimacy and emotional connections. He once told me that *No matter how beautiful a woman is, some man is tired of screwing her.*

Parents, care-takers, family members, and other adults need to be aware of the emotional displays of a child at puberty when it comes to

the child's interactions with individuals of their sexual preference. This is the prime-time where personality disorders begin to appear.

Part Three...The Play

ELEVEN

ATTACHMENT DISORDERS...IT'S GENERATIONAL

It's not that my mother never interacted with her children, she never interacted with anyone. She felt that people who made eye contact were insincere and people that showed self-esteem were creepy. I never laid eyes upon my aunts, uncles, cousins and other family members from her side of the family even though they all lived less than 50 miles away. I must wonder if my mother falls underneath the autism spectrum; a mild form: "According to the Autism Spectrum Resource Center, only 20% of people on the autism spectrum have classic autism. The overwhelming majority fall somewhere on the milder range of the spectrum."

However, my mother was able to pull off the making of a family and productive work-life while manifesting the negative aspects of a personality or pervasive developmental disorder. These are some factors in my mother's life that allowed my birth and growth into dysfunction: Born in a small, Midwestern town; a student in the 1950s where only the most severe learning disabled cases were diagnosed in the schools; lived as an adult in a time and place where housing was accessible and inexpensive; followed normal societal expectations to marry and have children soon after high school; settled down with a sociopath mate without strong systems in place to protect abused children and women; and access and ability to work at a low-skilled job with good pay and union protection. Another possibility with my mother is that when a developmental disorder goes undiagnosed and that person is forced to fend for him/herself, it manifests into Narcissism or Sociopathy.

PsychCentral.com: Short Autism Screening Test

(1) *I understand the feelings of others.*

(2) *I have difficulty in functioning in a group.*

(3) *I don't know how to act in social situations.*

(4) *I focus on details rather than overall ideas.*

(5) *I take things literally.*

(6) *I get upset when the way I like to do things suddenly changes.*

These items appear similar to Narcissistic Personality Disorder or Sociopathy. The key difference is that Narcissists know how to fake and manipulate what seems like appropriate social interactions (until their mask falls off), whereas those that fall underneath the autism spectrum do not. Also, Narcissists gain ego-energy with honeymoon periods, or impressing people, whereas those that fall on the autism spectrum do not know how to fake life and do not get energized by manipulating others to their side.

I believe attachment disorders emanate from the same miswiring, or even as a result of the same missing or non-firing brain matter, that was formed or not formed prenatally and up to around 12-years-old (I am not implying these are the same disorders only that they manifest from similar brain developments).

I can see myself falling on the autism spectrum. I have great difficulty in finding healthy people to bond with and will instead attach myself to unhealthy people. I have effectively learned to get along in society because of being and growing on my own since 18-years-old: I am able to intellectually understand that I should not live as a hermit because I've always been attached to the mental learning realm through constant studying and gaining degrees. However, I do not have an emotional understanding that clues me in that some people are just bad, or even evil. I attach and "love" without reason and throw myself down a sentimental and emotional rabbit-hole of trying to heart "save" the unsaveable. I cannot form healthy emotional bonding situations so I put myself in no-win situations as a way to keep myself somewhat "connected" to a world of human beings in which I am stuck. I "attach" to the unattachable and create emotional connections to struggles that I will never win. I even did this in my teaching career - somehow navigating toward the worst classrooms in the worst school districts. I suppose I do all this because there is a part of me that fears real connections.

True love or wisdom sees with perfect clarity the deficiencies of any form, and bends every effort to aid the indwelling life to liberate itself from trammels. It wisely recognizes those that need help, and those that need not its attention. Too much emphasis has been laid on that called love (interpreted by man, according to his present place in evolution) and not enough has been placed on wisdom (Bailey, *Letters On Occult Meditation,* 282).

A very important factor is my grandmother died when my mother was 12 years old whereby leaving my mother basically orphaned in the late 1950s. Not only did her mother die during the most important time of her little-girl life entering into puberty, but my mother claims her mother was never very loving anyway because of the family's poverty and the resulting stress. My mother described my grandmother as standing around all day crying because her daughter-in-laws were mean to her (my mother had brothers more than 20 years older than herself). My grandmother was diagnosed with stomach cancer and couldn't afford care so she was sent home to die. She was cooking, cleaning, and hanging laundry in agonizing pain a day before she took to bed and wailed out her last scream.

My mother has no problem-solving skills - without an emotional breakdown - and has difficulty discerning quality of relationships. Her brain, my father's brain, entwined in their miswiring...they found a meshing of their brains' unresponsiveness toward bonding with others, their children, and with one another...they were "partners" through their attachment disorders. But my father may have made, through his constant hateful rage fits, my mother's inability to bond with her children even more profound. Yet, another possibility is: she was mildly autistic but became narcissistic under the harmful energy of my sociopathic father.

Today, my mother can organize her thinking enough to see and understand traits of autism and relate to the factual information on the check-list whereas few can admit to being a Narcissist. There is no evil associated with seeing oneself as mildly autistic and those with Asperger's Syndrome can have areas of brilliance and expertise. My mother is very sharp in accounting and finances (though she never received formal training in these areas) and even proudly refers to herself as savant like. This explains why when I shared my experiences teaching students with autism and Asperger's Syndrome she would say, *Sometimes, I think I'm autistic.* She did not form social attachments, did not emotionally bond with her children, but yet she stayed with a sociopath for decades; she didn't have to emotionally attach to my father. He was a mere entity that generated an income to help maintain the house and to handle the kids (albeit brutally) so she wouldn't have to have emotional dealings with us. In actuality, my mother is not connected to her own soul so connecting to her children's would be impossible. You cannot see in others what you do not comprehend. Listen to the words that come out of people's mouths...it can be key to everything that happens with and around them.

My Sociopath came along when I was 40 years old and acted like my protector. I was tired: I had been fighting my way through more than two decades of college degrees, bad jobs, bad men, and exhausting ordeals to protect the animals of the earth and to care for the special education students. But mostly, I was suffering from the resulting devastation that the men in my life (men are destroyers of women), and people in general (women are destroyers of women), inflicted upon me and the animals I dearly loved. I threw caution-to-the-wind at 40 because I figured there was no way that I could do any worse than I had already done, therefore, things could only get better. I let My Sociopath take complete and instant possession of me and everything in my existence: I needed a guardian and I thought I found one. I wrongly believed that his taking control of everything in my world, of me, was a sign of intense love. I was in a fatigued emotional condition.

I settled for the worst men and special education classrooms because I was conditioned to not protect myself. This relates to why as a twelve year old I decided to wear white pants on the day that I first started my period. I gravitate toward situations that are unhealthy and no-win and I put myself through emotionally grueling tests by accepting the unhealthy and disloyal; pushing my integrity and emotional strength to the limits. I do this because I don't believe in the true safety of anything or in anyone. I quickly attach to the unhealthy, detach when it goes awry, return to test the same unhealthy situation, detach, return, repeat, self-punish. It's generational ...grandmother ... mother ... me.

My Sociopath came to the many parties that I hosted at Turk Narc's house accompanied by his depleted looking and stressed out Turkish wife. She was always in a high-strung state of agitation and aggression. However, seeing people in social gatherings, talking small-talk, being in a common and superficial environment with them is not really knowing someone. People display their social-face in public and their true nature shows in their curtained and intimate surroundings. True knowing only comes in intimate relationships with lovers, close family members and childhood friends we had when we were young and raw. My Sociopath appeared the calm and controlled, therefore, the good one, and his wife appeared the "crazy" one. Like all of us, I believed in opposites based upon surface appearances.

After rebounding from Turk Narc, I found myself complaining to a fellow Turk, or My Future Sociopath. He nodded and agreed with me that Turk Narc was bad and he was not liked by other Turks. I felt validated. We met for a drink at the nearby bar and this would be my demise. I thought I was safe: he was living with his girlfriend, the same girlfriend that he immediately moved in with after meeting her in an AOL chat-room and thus, abandoning his wife and daughter (he spread rumors that his wife was crazy). He was much older than me. I, again, mistakenly thought that older meant more evolved.

One drink is my Rosacea limit so I had two drinks. My Future Sociopath guided my willing and accommodating self into his rattling, 1960s, orange, VW Vanagon and drove all over Oceanside looking for a back street where we could have sex. I was 40 and I was madly desired by another Turkish man; my former 25 year old life picked right back up where I first met Turk Narc or when I still had hope. Sociopaths stake their claim to someone through sex first and foremost...they are no further evolved than cavemen (this is why it is crucial that women do not sleep with men until long after the initial lust period is over). I felt as if I didn't miss a beat. I was dismantled through time and the resulting ill-effects of malignant men and now I had a chance to win back my past. I fooled myself into believing I was right where I was meant to be. I expertly and successfully replaced one Turk with another, therefore, Turk Narc's devastation would be cleansed from my soul.

Shortly after meeting Turk Narc, all those years ago, he left for Turkey and I joined him there for a month (I paid for it myself). Things would be no different after having sex with My Future Sociopath. He claimed me as his own and he was going to Turkey. He was originally going to meet all the Turkish women that he was seeking out and controlling via Skype and MySpace, but now, upon meeting me, this part of his trip would be canceled. He told me within our first week together, after taking our relationship to the "drink at a bar and park to have sex" level, that he was leaving the live-in girlfriend after he returned from Turkey. I was The Chosen and I felt special.

A Narcissist creates an illusion of being in high-demand to entice a target and to further manipulate the target under his control with his words of her being The Chosen.

I was the prized white, educated, English-speaking American that could improve his social status, especially in Turkey. Turks admire Americans (though Turkey is not officially a Muslim Country - it is a secular republic - its aura and spiritual feel is that of suppression, dread, hostility, and soul suffering). Mostly, I was his proof, with regard to all his other failed relationships, that he was The Good One, The Desired, and all the other *crazy* exes were The Bad, The Lonely and The Undesired. He strutted me everywhere and plastered our pictures all over social media.

I knew from day one that I was on a crash course for disaster and yet, I still smiled in those pictures.

I arrived in Turkey, again, and this time for My Sociopath; I karmically returned to my old stomping grounds of my former self with Turk Narc. The street animals of Turkey were still suffering 15 years later; however, different was, My Sociopath was an animal lover; so he claimed. Finally, I will be with a Turk that cares about the suffering of the Turkish animals and I will be able to do good in this land that is so brutal to its creatures. My call to service filled me with an even greater delusion that My Sociopath was my soul mate that I had to discover by going through what I went through with Turk Narc.

I returned to my former life with a different Turkish man but this time around, I had a feeling that my spirit was directing my soul to accomplish what I didn't do all those years ago. All that time ago I was filled with inner terror and grief for the starving and suffering animals that were being kicked, discarded, and neglected by the Turks. Turk Narc told me back then, as I hurriedly walked these same streets trying desperately to keep up with his manic pace, that *There is NOTHING that can be done*. We, like all the hustling and scrambling Turks, scuttled forward and over the suffering animals to shop and to sit for hours in lunch or coffee places. My heart ached while in Turkey and since...leaving that harsh country with the images of the suffering ingrained in my mind.

Mysociopaths.blogspot.com, 4.29.2012:

Turkey is an amazing country full of the greatest ancient ruins in the world and Istanbul with its narrow, winding cobblestone streets, is the closest thing to Fairyland that survives today. But Turkey lacks True Beauty and Prosperity. When there are dying animals on their streets, not only is it void of Soulful-living and Beautiful people, but up from its ancient earth trodden by the Hittites to the Romans, Byzantines to Ottomans, percolates the rank of people that lost their inner compass for being true and powerful leaders.
END POST

My trip back to Turkey to meet with My Sociopath was for only eight-days. In those days, we carried dried cat and dog food around to various cities, villages, and into the ancient ruins to feed the hungry animals. Pet food is only found in specialty shops in Istanbul and other large cities and it is priced much higher than pet food in the US. Cat and dog food is considered a luxury item and thus there is an exploitation of those Turks who bond with the animals. Pet care is considered human weakness and frivolousness and the fact that I was with a Turk that went against this dogma energized me.

My soul was doing what it was supposed to be doing, and this time with a better man (so I fooled myself into believing). My Sociopath gave me an ultimatum during this time: I was to change my phone number so no one from my past could contact me. I was enthralled by such a self-assured man and was happy that he wasn't like Turk Narc: Emotionally Detached. My Sociopath was taking an active interest in my life and he was jealous of everyone, especially other men. I took this as a healthy emotional attachment: He loved me. Upon meeting his Turkish sister, she agreed and smiled approvingly: *I must change my phone number.* When I returned to the US., I immediately did as I was advised. Once again, I was the good girl that needed to do everything in accordance to the dictates of another to be *loved and protected*.

My Sociopath was to stay six weeks longer than me, but instead, he scurried back into our town within a few days after my return; he immediately left the girlfriend and moved in with me. He explained that we would have open email accounts and without delay, he was in my account. I had access to one of his but I felt strange looking, so I never did. I found out much later that he went back and read eight year old emails between Turk Narc and me. He forwarded these intimate and personal emails to his secret email accounts and to his many supporters. I am a well trained teacher and have difficulty in deleting records and a strong part of my soul is striving to keep track of my history so that I may dissect the pattern at another time. His email account, that I never looked at, was one account out of dozens that he used.

He cried the financial woes of his great generosity toward all the social media women, the woman he was just living with, and even his estranged daughter of several years past. His great giving nature and the fact that no one ever paid him back left him financially depleted. I felt sad for him and believed in our future: I gave him all my savings. This money soon disappeared on his obsession with the newest electronic gadgets and gizmos and specifically those that secretly audio and video recorded people, especially me, and tracking equipment. He took control of all my electronics by planting spyware, hiding auditory and visual recording devices everywhere in my home, and by hacking into all my bank accounts and even library account to monitor what books I was reading. (Update: My Sociopath recently started installing security cameras as a business. Be careful of individuals that have similar businesses. My Sociopath solicited my neighbor with an offer of free camera installations whereby he tried to direct a camera at my home.)

In the mean time, I left teaching, and plunged into his TV and electronic repair business so that we would prosper together as a couple. He told me of the Aegean Coast properties we would be buying. But he barely worked and instead talked all day to the wayward people drifting into the business to socialize and when they left, he hung out on facebook. Though I earned most of the business revenue, he locked me out of all our business accounts. The business earnings went to women he met on the internet, to compulsive shopping, to his support group members and to picking up tabs in bars and restaurants. In order to save us, I deferred my student loans, went without necessities and I ordered the little side dishes in restaurants. He went on Kaiser health insurance for $750.00/month and I went on welfare health insurance, or Medicare, by claiming that I was single with no income.

As I grew sicker and sicker, he went with me to community health clinics and sat there fully believing that I was a poor, single woman on welfare. Sociopaths marry but there is no "We" in their thinking...only Me vs. You. Sociopaths marry to keep you confined, serving and giving them sex. They, however, believe they are single, free without responsibility – unless so inclined (meaning that you are being "good") - and able to do what ever they want, when ever they want, to whom ever they want.

Needing a protector at this stage of my tired life with its worn out psyche ended up almost killing me. I became sick with *screaming high cortisol levels and fatigued adrenals.* I got full body edema, couldn't urinate and puffed up with pounds of water retention; the doctors could push their fingers into my body and see the rippling of waves throughout. I stopped eating but quickly gained 25 lbs. and all of it went to my upper body...again, the effects of the stress hormone, cortisol. This gave My Sociopath more of an excuse to ooze with Sociopath Hate toward me because I was now fat and ugly. The doctors told me I was in pre-stroke condition.

I was my mother...succumbing to a Sociopath because I didn't know how to form normal human attachments. I do bond with animals though because they are kind souls. My Sociopath ruminated in hatred toward my dogs because I loved them. If I dared show them affection, he oozed with Sociopath Venom so when he was around, I ignored them. He became outraged when I tried to pick up my small, white Chihuahua after he was accidentally injured in a closing door. He went into our business that day and spread rumors that *I had a sick fixation with my dogs and he didn't know what to do with me* (Red Flag: somewhat "healthy" men do NOT reveal so-called "truths" about other people, especially intimate partners, in public ways). This happened in my home, soon after we got together, after I gave him all my money and while I was paying all the bills.

I saw what was lurking in my home soon after our quick and lustful trip to Turkey, the treachery that would destroy me and hate innocent creatures for receiving love from me. Most any woman would have immediately gotten rid of him but I remained frozen in thought...lost in time...*I would fix "it" because I was wrong to love my dogs*...I was responsible for creating his evil-energy so I would tiptoe to not aggravate the hostile force that was my creation. The slimy serpent took over my home...the home that was supposed to have been my safe place after Turk Narc. Not only did I not welcome safety into my life, but I attracted danger.

We do NOT know someone by casually socializing with them; we are lulled into a lazy-minded sense of security. This false sense of security is particularly dangerous for those of us who do not properly process red flags in a relationship. It is best to meet someone through a productive activity (group, event, cause), form a long-term friendship based upon the work involved...if destined, a mutual and intimate love will further evolve. (Update: there is a dangerous trend where women and men, who went to high school or college together, are reuniting on facebook to idealize and glamorize "what could have been." These people are leaving their long term partners and marriages to run across the state, and even country, to chase a fantasy, "ideal," superficial image to only find out 1-3 months later that their lives are ruined.)

However, be leery, My Sociopath told me that *he pretends to not be interested in women, not to notice them at all, and this intrigues women more...she feels rejected and wants to win his attention*; reverse psychology. Some Socios/Narcs know this maneuver!

Since a possible diagnosis of mild autism does not seem to offend or scare people like being told they are Narcissistic or Sociopathic, why not administer suspected Narcissists the "Short Autism Screening Test" as a non-threatening prescreening tool? It can then be backed up with further analysis regarding the person's relationship patterns and the residual aftermath of those in their past and the condition of those in their current life. I took it and was not at all offended because I know that I have social bonding issues but I also know that I never harm people. My mother is not offended by possibly being autistic because she doesn't see herself as harmful. She is very detached from the effects of her actions and cause and effect.

My mother saying that she thinks she is autistic was the key information that I needed to look back at the human destruction she creates around her and therefore, I was able to understand that not only was my father a sociopath, but it is likely she is mildly autistic, borderline, narcissistic or sociopathic herself. As a result, I started understanding why I've allowed myself to be harmed over and over again and why I lack healthy emotional skills when it comes to intimate relationships.

No one is ever going to heal our wounds that we carry over from our past and into a relationship with them. The only protection that we will get, the only healing that we can discover, is within and manifested by us. The adults that carry childhood abuse and trauma within cannot look for outer sources for their completion but must work a little every day at filling their own wounds with inner-security. We must train ourselves to find a healthy and productive path of living. This means to not fall under the power of intensely stimulating, too wildly energetic, manically operating sources, and to not allow the other extreme into our lives...someone who is dormant or not growing.

We must strive for resiliency in all that we do and attract by finding people and situations that are steadfast, without drama, and nurturing to higher growth. Until we learn how to have healthy attachments, we should go inward to find our own strength to work toward our own growth and development. We must train ourselves to act from thinking, not feeling.

TWELVE

SOCIOPATH CONTROL

My father controlled his children's adolescent development. He was vicious and cruel when we started caring about the way we looked; he bullied, mocked, ridiculed and enacted punishments during this important phase of our development. We were not permitted to shower or wash our hair and he even made our appearance look funny. At random times, he forced me to remove my contacts and wear big, broken glasses with tape across the nose-bridge. He called us names such as pig, duck foot, slob, and weirdo. This control applied to my mother in strange ways. He did not allow her to drink water when she was thirsty and many years later she threw this strange fact at me when I tried to bring up my childhood: *Well, what about me, I wasn't allowed to drink water!* If my mother did respond to our mention of his bad treatment, she threw her mistreatment back in response. My brothers and I grew up believing that my mother lived our same childhood.

Whenever My Sociopath created a dramatic situation between us, I refused to go into his dying business. On the days that I didn't go in, he found another easy and willing target to replace me. He didn't need anyone to replace anyone, this was a one-man shop, but **Sociopaths cannot be alone!** My Sociopath managed to lure in a drained woman in her 50s who was unhealthy and barely making life on her own. She proved to be desperate for attention from The Grand Turk with a Business.

My Sociopath *saved* this depleted woman by offering her $4.00/hr under-the-table money, but in addition to her unemployment, this was good for her situation; for hanging out in a failing business and just fulfilling a Sociopath's need for attention and stimulation. My Sociopath has a continuing flow of replaceable people-parts in his surroundings and he recycles through all of us to access the energy he needs. Sociopaths cannot go inward, not even when they are supposed to be working. If a Sociopath were to stay engaged in his work effort, he must be in a highly stimulating environment with people milling about and around him. I bet not many Sociopaths are writers, philosophers, librarians or scientists in laboratories.

The person that took over my office chair on those many days of my retreat was Karen. I wasn't knowledgeable about personality disorders but understood that My Sociopath could never be alone, and that Karen was a part of his incessant need for attention and stimulation, so I never took it out on her. I just used the days that Karen sat in the crumbling-down garage business with My Sociopath chaotically lurking about, as a day for my rest and recovery at home. Plus, he cruelly condemned me when I paid attention to my dogs so I used these days to care for them and to allow the essence of their pure and forgiving souls to absorb within me. I was physically, emotionally and mentally sickened by the evil, soul-absorber in my midst and I needed my dogs to offset this.

However, My Sociopath and I planned another trip to Turkey and Karen would be taking care of our business for more than a month. Since I thought about the greater good, or my being in Turkey to do animal rescue work, I agreed to help prepare Karen for the running of the business for this extended time. Karen and I met in the tiny, haphazardly built *office*. Sociopaths never plan anything out; the office was built too small and nothing fit inside. She and I sat smashed together as I patiently showed her how to use our accounting system.

My Sociopath stood nearby. His body facing the opposite direction of Karen and me but his eyeball, in the eye closest to us, was stuck in its outside corner: It was looking at us! Many birds, reptiles, amphibians and fish have eyes on the side of their head because they must watch out for predators. Humans have eyes that face forward because we are dominant on the food chain and do not have to worry about being eaten. Sociopaths are unique creatures in that though they are predators, they are extremely paranoid, and think everyone else is out to eat them.

After our session was over and Karen walked away happy that I wasn't as scary as My Sociopath led her to believe, he hissed at me with the cold-blast of a Midwest winter: "**I bet you felt powerful, didn't you!**" He stormed away. Chills consumed my bones, a frost penetrated my aura. My Sociopath turned into death because I felt genuinely free and spirited and someone positively responded to me. He wanted me locked inside his breathless death chamber and for a moment in time, I unchained myself. I had to be in a lower position to him in the eyes of his supporters, actually, I was to be in no position at all. Sociopaths want you completely and forever powerless. Not only did I exude my own sense of self and power but I later found out My Sociopath was enacting a heavy smear-campaign against me and I defied the smear. Upon our return from Turkey, he got drunk and had sex with Karen. Things are meant to be just as they are...we just don't realize this at the time. My Sociopath bought a home with Karen while we were married and she gives him grief to this day.

You are not permitted to feel or show any self-confidence, or a self-assured command of a subject, or the positive directing of your knowledge or wisdom, even when this may benefit The Sociopath. This was the total annihilation of my inner-being and dousing of any flame of my manifesting light: I am a natural teacher, a professionally educated one and I completed a year of accounting courses for his business.

A Sociopath will destroy a target even if that target is instrumental in propelling him forward. I was always a spirited learner and especially enthused teacher...as a child I led the neighborhood kids through dirt piles, trails, and into the tops of trees. We are not allowed to exude soul. Sociopaths are fearful of humans with self-directed souls and that is why they target those who readily hand over their light. When you fade, he thrives...he no longer has to worry about you attracting good people and situations that threatens his sense of control.

The Sociopath targets and annihilates victims who are not in control of their soul and its directed higher purpose. He preys upon those dehumanized from childhood, past relationships, or other traumas, and those who never learned to take command of their physical, emotional and mental bodies. The Sociopath steals and occupies humanness...robbing life away from those who allow it.

My Soul has already died of loneliness. I'm really dead. The only reason I shout and agitate so much is that I am afraid of the corpse that is my soul (Szepes).

THIRTEEN

A WORKHORSE FOR NARCISSIST CRUMBS

When growing up in an abusive household, you learn to keep the peace, walk on eggshells, or hideaway and lay-low...to make yourself small. My brothers and I scattered into our bedrooms when my father came home from work. Any wounded animal will run and hide when seeing the force that hurt it. However, there were consequences to our instinctual and normal behavior: My father had a screaming fit that we were "hiding" from him. He forced us out of our bedrooms... beating us as we moved down the narrow hallway...bodies smashed together, one striking as the other squeezed themselves small. We then had to sit in the cold and stark family room...void of colors, paintings, or cutesy objects of any kind.

I read Victorian literature and Charles Dickens writes of the mistreatment of children and orphans. The girl children are abused by being locked away in attics and in bedrooms and deprived meals and what was then considered luxurious treatments such as baths, perfumes, nice clothes and hair brushings. Even in these cruel depictions, I don't think I've ever read of a little girl being beaten. This intrigues my mind because I am always dissecting my life by way of trying to figure out my karma: A little girl beaten in Midwestern 1980s by a sociopath father. My father never beat my younger brother. My older brother is not his and I realized too, recently, that I look nothing like my father and I resemble no family member on his side of the family. Nice to think that I might have a different father...out there...somewhere.

Eventually, my father grew tired of our sitting in the family room that was as narrow as that hallway. We were allowed to disperse outside, but still not allowed in our bedrooms, because that would defeat the entire purpose of his punishment regarding our initial *hiding*. Freedom and relief was obtained in the outside and on one of these days, I scrambled up my favorite tree. I fell out of that tree so hard that my stomach went through my back and indented into the ground...breath knocked out of me, body bruised, sprained and immobile. I remained quiet, still, staring up at the sky. I never cried out for help...I didn't want to be a burden. Hours later the neighbor noticed purple mound on top of green grass. He gently loomed over me, blocking the view of my cloud people and animals, and asked me if I was okay. I meekly smiled and said, "yes." As night approached, I crawled home and into bed. I walked with a severe limp for months and it took another visiting aunt to ask my mother if I was okay. My mother never noticed my swollen and bent body.

My destiny was firmly understood when my father told me that I was too old to live at home and a "loser in life" when I turned 18. I would have to do all the sacrificing to be in a relationship because not only was I "old" (I was now in my 20's), but I could be discarded. When I got involved with Turk Narc, I *laid low* and *hid* so that I would be a woman without wants or needs. I didn't want to be a burden...a hassle. I didn't know my power as a young, beautiful, smart, educated, working-to-support-myself woman and I didn't know that a good man would have loved and protected me. It's logic: younger woman gets security and older man gets fun and a feeling of youth and energy. Women with fewer qualities have older men in the palms of their hands but this Narcissist made me powerless and I catered to his needs. I was defective and didn't even understand that I was young, let alone beautiful and smart. I allowed older men to use me; I devalued myself. This is my twisted fate: If I came from less destructive parents, I would not have only expected great treatment, but required it from an older man...any man, anyone. I was a blank canvas of spilled paint that permitted my latent artistic form to be smeared in place to sustain the egos of others.

I was attending my last week of classes, before graduating, when I crossed the path of Professor Turk Narc on campus. He was tall, dark and menacing. He looked like Dracula and what woman doesn't have a fantasy about Dracula? He cast the predator stare upon me as I apprehensively, per my usual gait that lacked assertiveness, walked upon him. I used to walk with my head tilted slightly downward and only recently realized that this isn't being cute but it's being a target. I had to consciously train myself to walk all the way up and more determined. He stopped me and commented on the bracelet I was wearing. He knew he snared a young girl without ego...it's the lack of eye contact, the non-assertive speech, the undetermined gait, the lowered head.

Narcissists seek those without ego because it is primal...it is the survival response system in their reptilian brain: *There can only be one ego in my relationship and it is MY ego!* Narcissists have an uncanny ability to find egoless women. Ego in the sense of healthy ego that gives you a foundation for who you are and your positive role on this planet. There cannot be two egos in a relationship with a Narcissist because a second ego is a direct threat to his survival: A woman with a healthy ego cannot be controlled or manipulated; she will not shine upon the Narcissist with admiration but will expect the Narcissist to shine upon her.

Turk Narc boasted to me about a very old professor that had sex with one of his young students in the backseat of his car out in the college parking lot and they eventually married. I pretended to be naive and said, "Oh, I'm sure she has a nice, easy-going life." Turk Narc shot a death glance at me and proclaimed that *she works all day for him, she does EVERYTHING.* I calmly stated that *this was odd because young women are usually provided for and nurtured by older men...That is why they marry older men.* Turk Narc's mask fell off and he showed his disdain for me and all women.

Narcissists and Sociopaths hate women, especially women with healthy egos! I showed an ego that expected something from him...I showed an ego of a younger woman with an older man. I was only to be the younger, easygoing, fun-loving, sex-giving, insecure workhorse. He didn't have to provide me with anything...anything that is but a penis and cheap wine. Within six months of knowing Turk Narc he proclaimed, "All women are bitches." I internalized this as my job to be his perfect woman without wants, without needs.

I allowed men to enter my life and claim me as a sexual partner with my fulfilling all their *wife*, *friend* and *worker* needs and my requiring very little in return.

"The muse is supposed to be the powerful one in the relationship, capable of granting or withholding favors as she pleases. Here the muse has become powerless while her beneficiary prospers — It's a strange image" (Leinen, *Reflections on a Homeless Muse*).

(Blog post regarding Leonard Cohen's disregard for his muse, Suzanne Verdal, who inspired his most covered hit song *Suzanne*. Suzanne is homeless.)

Narcissists do not take care of women but only want women for fun. There is no adult partnership with him. He comes first, you come second...and sometimes, not at all. Turk Narc bought a new home after we met. I was now in a graduate program, teaching students with aggressive behavior disorders (the last field I should have been in) and participating in pet adoption shows. All the while, I spent the entire summer doing construction work on his new home: on ladders holding large garbage can lids as I scraped his popcorn ceilings with the asbestos clumps falling down past my open mouth and nostrils and into this heavy and awkward catching device; picking weeds for 8 hours a day; lifting and transporting rocks in my broken down car for his rock garden; cooking deluxe meals from scratch for him and his Apath crowd of supporters. He fed me a salad, poured me cheap wine, lit me a Dunhill, showed me some of that sexual prowess and I was grateful. Actually, deep down, I felt this was too much and I was undeserving. I asked him five years in a row to help me decorate my classroom before the first day of school, and every year he was too busy.

During this time, Turk Narc asked me to move in with him but I had to keep all my pets outside. I was now 27 and could live with a much older professor near the ocean. In all my lacking self-esteem mind and body, I said, "No, my pets have to be inside and we can build an enclosed patio to make this easier." I volunteered to pay for it...he refused...I declined his offer (I only lived with him a couple of times in a span of 15 years and they were brief situations between my own home rentals or purchases). Narcissists never compromise for others. I was driven, despite my childhood, to stay on the right path for my higher calling. I can look back in astonishment of my Will to protect the animals whereas many young women would have discarded their pets for a Great Ottoman Professor...not to mention, he was tall and he was Dracula.

Will, or purpose, must be accessed through self-esteem issues.

Turk Narc checked the oil on my beaten-down Geo Metro that hauled his rocks and he left the hood unfastened. That hood flew off as I was driving on the freeway following him to go to his house to work for the day. I almost died and I almost killed many others. It was my responsibility, not his, to search Oceanside junkyards to find a hood replacement. I dealt with the mean, old, grumbling junkyard guys and eventually found a new hood that I paid to get installed. Turk Narc never offered to help nor to pay for the tragedy that almost cost me my life...he only smiled at my funny life of near freeway deaths and junkyard stories.

I was a young and injured girl with an Old Narcissistic Man. I retreated into my wounds and Turk Narc surveyed, dug for and located more of my artifacts so that his brilliant, excavator personality could feel powerful. He was my mother's and father's wounds and this is what I attracted. I crouched behind his superiority with my inferiority in order to survive in his big man's world. He threw crumbs at my lack of self-worth and I gobbled up those crumbs.

We accept the treatment that we believe we are worth through our childhood-brainwashing that grows into records playing, rather skipping, in our brains; continually gravitating toward the same abusive settings. When you look inside and see your true beauty and worth and realize the brainwashing that you were programmed into believing...when you stop the record playing, you stop accepting crumbs.

Making yourself small will attract Narcissists and others with personality disorders; it is manifested insecurity. See your soul and know where it stands: This is your Will and Purpose. This means making yourself large based upon authentic and genuine motivations and following through with your plan. Your soul is never insecure or emotionally reactive and it always knows who it is and where it is going; only your personality flutters and splatters with insecurity and indecision.

Sociopaths Make Us Carry All The Burden

When I was with Turk Narc, I made a constant joke about my life and the "bad luck" that seemed to follow me. He relished in my self-deprecating talk and would grin and light up. Disturbed individuals thrive off of our misfortunes, hardships, insecurities and the resulting confusion in our minds. Our uncertainties give a Sociopath or Narcissist reassurance in their own power and further pumps them up to loom down upon us. Run from a person that enjoys your misfortune, even if you are the one making a joke about it. This relates to Right Speech. Self-deprecation is used in humor, to show modesty and for tension release. However, we should be careful in using it around unfamiliar social situations and with predator type of people where it may be used against us.

I volunteered to pet sit Monkey during the San Diego County Wildfires of 2007 for a co-worker. The teacher that worked in the classroom next to mine had to evacuate his home. I came home from work one day and Monkey was dead. Turk Narc loomed behind me as I walked toward this horrifying discovery. In shock, I turned to him and asked what happened. He stood stone cold, silent, pursed and thin lips, mouth lines smashed together, darkness lingering in place of his aura...he said nothing, not a word. Shaking and in a trance I called my co-worker to explain, to give no explanation, nothing...*Monkey died*. I spent the rest of the school-year shrunken into myself, growing even older in my classroom next door to Monkey's former companion. The students smiled at me for being such a nice person to pet sit their favorite teacher's dog...the result of my "kindness" never revealed....the breath knocked out of me...I merely smiled back.

I spent years after crying over this and blaming myself...*I fed Monkey something bad before I went to work...there was poison in the yard*...Turk Narc allowed me to carry the burden. Only victims feel compelled to try to explain things, figure things out, put the pieces of the puzzle together. Narcissists are left free, clear, and able to sleep soundly at night. Turk Narc could have taken this weight off my shoulders by being a man or telling the truth to my co-worker and me about Monkey, but why when he had a much younger, kinder, softer and more guilt-ridden object do the work.

Narcissists sabotage and destroy our environment because of their intensely self-centered regard for their own life and surroundings. In addition, they are so intensely focused on obtaining sex, adoration and other gratifications from people that they neglect our safety and everything else in our lives. It is difficult to pin down his responsibility when chaos surrounds us because of his cold emotionalism. We confuse his non-reaction as his measured, emotional control and of his stoic innocence and as a result, we blame ourselves and think everything happens because of our inadequacy, bad luck and bad karma. The Narcissist gleams with pleasure as we disintegrate into our own morose sense of self-hatred and self-blame. One thing for certain, he gets away with harming our environment because he simply does not feel that he needs to answer to anything and that he has a right to remain silent. The right to remain silent may hold true in situations involving the police but it does not hold true in intimate relationships or during a crisis. Narcissists freeze when reality is forced upon them and when they cannot back away.

When he is silent during serious relationship issues, he is being abusive. If a Narcissist is not lying, if he is not telling a half-truth, he is quiet.

Because The Narcissist never takes responsibility, we are left carrying the scars, burdens, regrets, and traumas for the entire relationship, for everything he does, for years into the future...

Narcissists travel lightly upon this earth because we are the ones that carry their burden:

1. **Be Stoic in Speech.**

   Practice good speech in your everyday life and in the smallest of interactions.

   Don't put yourself down in speech with others. Our presentation is illuminated within the smallest details that we project.

2. **Develop clear vision. The seeing of what is really there and not what you wish to be there.**

   Use your intellect to determine appropriate and inappropriate human reactions.

   If someone doesn't offer an explanation when asked, this may be an indication of guilt, not innocence.

3. **Use your conscientiousness toward good causes not empty ones.**

   It is not always your duty to make everything right. Some things are not your responsibility.

FOURTEEN

THE DISCARD, THE SMEAR-CAMPAIGN

We likely came to the realization that we were with a Sociopath or Narcissist during The Discard. This is when he appears the most inhumane, sadistic, brutal, callous and void-like...an empty vessel. His mask has completely fallen off and he represents death. The Discard is when The Narcissist makes a clean and abrupt break from an intimate partner in a cruel and inhumane way, without taking responsibility and without feeling remorse. He does this with drama: temporary restraining orders (TROs) or divorce papers filed rashly; ending the lease with your landlord without your knowledge or input; abruptly starting another intimate relationship; moving out with a new girlfriend leaving you stuck with the house payment and bills; etc. He takes no responsibility for our immediate survival of our now wrecked lives that he caused on a physical, emotional, mental and financial level. We are left ill, or homeless, or in poverty. The Narcissist simply does not care...he moved on to his next target.

He never creates closure with previous relationships and immediately jumps into a new relationship leaving the previous target shocked. This extreme and non-human cold detachment is what propels many of us to inquire and research into the possibility that he has some type of mental or personality disorder, and what leads us down the road to discovering what a sociopath or narcissist is. These words may have been previously whispered or loudly proclaimed to us by friends while with this person, but we shrugged it off with an air of denial. The *Sociopath* or *Narcissist* words are not new to our ears; only now, upon the cruel discard, do we bring these words forth to consciousness.

Being a disposable and easily replaceable object is traumatic and this is why narcissistic abuse penetrates all levels of our existence and recovery takes so long. Even before the final discard, we lived and breathed in an atmosphere of knowing we were replaceable and this looming reality is what made us highly reactive and nervous. Every human (and animal) has a right to hold a special place of honor in his/her environment and when we are treated as a replaceable component, we fester in fear, anxiety and insecurity.

A friend who is 25 years older than me called Turk Narc a Narcissist. I repeated this word to him and he shrugged it off that my friend was old, lonely and bitter because of her lack of man. I immediately dismissed my friend's insight. We live in a world where women shun aside the wisdom of other women to be with and protect bad men. I now realize that some women remain single in their older years because of the great despair they experienced with bad men when they were younger. Perhaps these "bitter" acting women once loved with all their hearts and were exploited for their kind offerings?

Years past Turk Narc, My Sociopath left me physically sick from being in fight-or-flight for so long and emotionally and psychologically depleted from endless mind-games, turning-the-tables, word-salad, setting me up to emotionally crack in front of people, and ruining all my financial and hard work contributions. He was now pulling the Final Discard by leaving me financially destitute after I gave him all my money and savings (tens of thousands of dollars) and donating endless work hours for our business without ever taking pay or tending to my own basic needs. Turk Narc was detrimental but My Sociopath was dangerous. I went from bad to worse. I allowed my dignity to be taken from me, my reputation to be ruined, and my humanness to be stolen. I started to wonder if I could ever handle a healthy relationship free of drama and chaos with a healthy man. Perhaps this would bore me?

We must analyze our own personality tendencies or those selfish things we do to satiate our low-level physical, emotional and mental needs to achieve attention, stimulation and desire fulfillment; the tendencies that do not lead to our growth. Narcissists operate low-level personality desires but even non-narcissists can fall into this trap.

Step by step and stage by stage, we construct that Path just as the spider spins its thread. It is that "way back" which we evolve out of ourselves; it is that Way which we also find and tread (Bailey, *Education in The New Age, 7*).

The final discard is what jolted my brain into a frightful state and impelled it to go backward in time, to retrace my steps down the crazy path of turmoil and destruction that he led me on and toward my quest to search the internet for answers. I realized that I was reliving my mother and father. I was half my mother...half my father. All my education...all the miles that I moved away to escape it, I had been living it all along. Turk Narc was my mean, cold, punishing father; I was with him to get the approval that I never received from my father. He smelled like my father, had his similar hair and skin coloring and embodied his dark aura. My Sociopath played out the same behaviors as my mother: The poor victim that never does anything wrong; everyone else is to blame. Both men were experts at camouflaging their destruction with an air of cool, calm, emotional detachment.

The final discard with My Sociopath was NOT a loss of love. He stole from me. Sociopaths believe what's yours is mine, what's mine is mine, what's ours is mine. All or Nothing. When he is with you and you are under his control, he will 'share' with you his belongings within very strict and confining limits, though you hand over everything of yours to him. During The Discard he robs you of everything and tells everyone that you stole from him. Or, if by rare chance, it is determined that he took something of yours, he will present a story that you are *bad, and owe him, and that is why he had to take from you.*

Just like a Sociopath does not respect our personal boundaries, he does not, and will not, even after The Discard, respect our property. He believes he has a right to ALL and we are not separate, living, human entities and therefore, we should not have anything that we independently have or love....outside him. This is even evident before The Discard: My Sociopath broke every treasure that I owned...those heart items that I brought back from my travels. He hung up my stone Italian cross on the patio lattice with a piece of tape. When it immediately fell to shatter into crumbled dust he scolded my shock with defiant arrogance because he was "only trying to help." He claimed every pile of crushed memories was nothing but an accident and I had no right to be upset; I was overreacting. Sociopaths are careless with our life and our belongings. However, if the opposite were to occur, or our accidentally hurting something he owns, he would fly into a rage and assault us for our inadequacy.

We not only beat ourselves up for our non-perfection but we succumb to relationships where we allow others to torment us for not being perfect.

When we crumble, The Narcissist puts extra energy into vitalizing his support group. He needs their protection more when he is going through yet another breakup. This is the most important time of his life, another breakup, where he needs to shine as the Great Victim Man to distract the supporters in seeing the fact that he destroyed another relationship. This component of The Discard also sends the now former target into emotional chaos: *He is loved by everyone...How can this be! Why doesn't anyone else see?*

The Sociopath controls the ending, therefore, he controls you. In my situation, I was filing for divorce against My Sociopath and he begged me to hold off so we could "talk." I did just as he requested. He turned around and quickly filed for divorce against me. Though it does not matter who files for divorce first (perhaps in cases of venue only), this maneuver gave My Sociopath a great first impression to excuse away another failed relationship.

It provided him with another 'I'm a Victim of an Abusive Wife" card with his supporters and his future targets. He cried the "I had to divorce the wife" to gain his next victim even quicker than his per usual. This activates the similar *poor boy* psychology in women toward widower men.

The Sociopath manages a discard even if you are the one leaving him. He has to be in charge of the final steps and when he is in charge of anything regarding you, you are ruined. **Do not let anyone control your endings!** The Sociopath pulls a twisted maneuver of mass manipulation at what becomes his special brand of discard. He then immediately acts as if you never existed and are not a human being. In actuality, he is not acting...in his miswired brain you are a damaged, unworthy and obsolete object.

Your existence was only in the superficial material form; you were an object and your form was *loved* only when you were providing a high to energize him. We did not exist on a real, human being level because Sociopaths cannot emotionally attach; we existed through our offerings. These offerings included giving him attention, ego-stroking, adoration, work and labor for his betterment and comfort, endless financial sacrifices and contributions, cooking, cleaning, caretaking and submission to his control and manipulation. When your offerings end, his true nature shows and The Discard is quick and cruel. You are now horrendous to him and he convinced everyone else of this.

Another cruel part of The Discard is his refusal to apologize or to offer any explanation...closure. I will take an insincere apology over no apology because at the least, I receive a moment of validation...my nervous system receives a moment of calm. If you fight for your rights, or demand answers, he will get the police or courts involved. He will throw you and your children out of your home, file a restraining order or call the police on you. You were the one that continually left, repeatedly returned, and now you are THE DISCARDED. You may now have a TRO on the public court-index.

No matter if his TRO filing proves to be frivolous, the ineffectual court system in the US and other countries leaves his filing on the court-index. The court-index does not notate the very pertinent "frivolous" ruling; only that it was filed and a third party would have to go to the courthouse to pull the original file to see the final ruling. Who will take the time and energy to do that? You now have a TRO filed under your name. Talk about lasting scars of The Narc/Socio relationship. I am a public school teacher and private math tutor so there is a good chance that administrators/fellow teachers and parents will do a background check on me. What turned out to be a frivolous TRO filing happened to me. Turk Narc did it. The reward I get for having a history of attracting, staying with, repeatedly forgiving disloyal and unforgiving acts, and returning multiple times to bad men.

If you're in a pattern of attracting unhealthy relationships, your previous Discard Remnants will be used against you by other bad people. A Sociopath unearths your entire existence upon meeting you (I did not detect this in those who were primarily Narcissistic and BPD). My Sociopath did an immediate internet search on me and his vulture brain knew how to use the online court-index as his main source of information. He discovered the TRO with Turk Narc. I explained it was ruled frivolous by the judge yet he still ran down to the courthouse the next day to pull the file. To my shock he told me what he did and ridiculed Turk Narc for the embarrassment he caused himself in filing this (the judge made such condemning remarks that were noted in the file). I felt redeemed despite this creepy gesture from My Sociopath at the beginning of our intimate relationship. However, he still told his crowd of supporters that I had a TRO without adding the important facts of what he discovered himself. This worked to automatically disenfranchise me from my social surroundings. I was immediately set up for failure...no matter what he did to me in the coming future, I had no defense because I was the one with the TRO. The more severe The Personality Disordered, the sooner you are set up for the smear-campaign.

The Smear-Campaign Tactics

A Narcissist destroys you before and after The Discard. When a person is murdered, that's it, one act and they are dead. There is not a continual ruination of the dead person's body. However, a Narcissist keeps ruining you, your reputation, your livelihood, your chances to rebuild and to get back on your feet. You essentially become the walking dead and that's what he wants to happen to you: He wants you *dead,* without risking jail or putting his "victim boy" persona into question, so he employs other methods to keep you from striving:

1. Spreads rumors about you involving your mental health, family dynamics, past relationships, weaknesses and fears. Twist around personal stories you told him to make you look damaged, unstable and defective. Does this by acting concerned.

2. Steals family members and friends, infiltrates your groups and social networks and turns your neighbors against you. He does this by using a sorrowful and confused expression and saying such lines as: *I'm concerned...I don't know what to do with her...I'm trying my best.*

3. Sabotages your job by creating chaotic and confusing situations so you are physically, emotionally and mentally weakened. Makes anonymous calls to your boss or writes fake bad reviews about you online.

4. Hacks into your email and social media accounts or creates an identical or very similar account to yours, poses as you and ruins your relationships.

5. Sends strange emails to you indicating how bad you are and other items that don't make sense. He is blind-copying his supporters.

6. Secretly records you after he instigates you into reaction.

7. Sneaks into your home and car with extra keys that he kept to look for evidence that you are in another relationship or in a weakened condition (takes pictures of your less than tidy house or even alcohol bottles).

8. If you have children, he will manipulate a child into acting as his spy to report *bad* things about you.

9. Changes the timeline of your new relationship that you were cheating on him with this new person while still with him.

10. If you remain single, he will portray you as defective and unlovable.

Your friends never really liked you anyway; they always liked him more and felt sorry for him to have had to tolerate you. You were only a problem in the eyes of your family and because he sacrificed so much in the loving care of you, your family is in debt to him. You are to be left penniless because you never worked or contributed anyway...he worked constantly for your ingratitude and his financial messes are your fault.

Narcissists recruit their new target to destroy you. My Sociopath beamed as he told me his last girlfriend helped him write fake, bad reviews on ratemyprofessor against his ex-wife. He has terrible English writing skills and would convince the newest target to do his writing and advocating for him...especially if it involved destroying someone who was *horrible* toward him. To My Sociopath, this girlfriend that was helping him destroy his ex-wife, was not only showing him intense and unconditional love, but she was validating him in the grand lie that the mother of his daughter was The Bad One, and he was The Good One. This girlfriend, that was an enabling destroyer of the innocent, was a heroin and savior in the eyes of a Sociopath.

For anyone that is a teacher or a public worker, when one student or customer says something bad about you (even a fake person/fake review), many others, especially those non-thinking with the common and prevalent human trait of mob-mentality, will use that as an impetus or evidence to find more bad about you. Just like the filing of TROs that are frivolous: A downward spiral of negativity and destruction occurs surrounding the person that these filings, reviews, and gossips are thrust upon. The mother of his child is basically ruined even as a part-time instructor. Sociopaths and Narcissists thrive when we are continually destroyed. Therefore, they are the *Publicly Proven Winners* and we are the *Publicly Proven Losers*.

Gossiping causes the ruination of people everywhere, throughout time and place, but there is no person more destroyed by gossip than a former target of a Narcissist. Narcissists are gossips and their Apath enablers are equally nasty gossips. The people that end up being an enabler of a Narcissist are low-level, small-minded and gossip is a typical part of this personality type. Apaths are the people that stand for nothing and fall for everything. They don't have a backbone and don't stand up for the little guy; they don't discern right from wrong, good from bad and they go with the flow or with the most exciting person that creates a high-energy vortex in their social surroundings, i.e., The Narcissist or Sociopath.

Men have a moral obligation to protect a woman's reputation during and after his intimate involvement with her. Men are protectors, women are nurturers. A decent man does not talk in such slanderous and gossipy ways about women he had intimate relationships with. Good people don't do this to their former or current lovers. And more glaringly dangerous are those men who slander and destroy the reputation of the mother of their child. There will come a day when dangerous men are easily identified by the way they speak about women, especially their exes. There will come a day when good men are identified by the way they protect all women, even their exes. (Not all females are of good quality and void of innocence...however, this does not mean that they should be publicly ruined.)

The Smear-Campaign is his way of leaving us de-powered forever. This is no different from when we were in a relationship with him: he de-powered us then. I let my power go because I went against all intuition and instead operated from a false belief that things would be okay. We put ourselves in his trap for various reasons such as having financial problems, needing a place to stay or a helper for the children, or during a life transition. It could be for reasons that go deeper and unrealized to you even at this reading: depression; overall fatigue from fighting life on your own or with unhealthy partners; a diagnosed or undiagnosed physical or mental condition; previous years of destructive life-patterns; self-sabotaging because of unresolved trauma or feelings of unworthiness; or just *I Want to Be The Best Woman He's Ever Had* ego.

To Transcend from the Smear-Campaign:

"*I will keep Silence. I will perform only my own task. I will not discuss any personality. I will achieve non-attachment. I will practice discernment. I will retain a quiet mind. I am a Cup, a Flame, a Sword, for I am Truth*" (An Elder Brother, *Unsigned Letters from an Elder Brother*).

Narcissist Abuse & TRO Filings: Court Responsibility

1. **The Family Court System needs to change the Restraining Order Process and look closely at the person filing the restraining order to examine if there is real FEAR behind their filing.** I can detect real fear in a person, as opposed to a manufactured fear...Why can't the courts? People with personality disorders will file TROs for nuisance situations only. There needs to be a protocol where real fear for one's life and dealing with a nuisance are differentiated. In some cases, "nuisance situations" are the refusal of the personality disordered to properly resolve issues and this should not result in a TRO filing.

2. **When a Temporary Restraining Order is granted, and then proven frivolous or not given Permanent Status, the filing needs to be removed from the online court-index.** Some people have a history of attracting unhealthy relationships and will

subsequently attract those that may harm us by using TROs, even those not granted Permanent, to inflict further harm.

3. **The Courts need to fine and hold accountable people who file TROs that are proven unnecessary.** This person needs to be red-flagged in the court-index or other computer recording system for their frivolous filing. This holding of accountability includes the office worker that helped the person process the initial TRO.

Narcissists use and manipulate the law to their I'm a Victim advantage: Crying the innocent victim results in their frivolous filings of restraining orders and police reports. This is The Narcissist's way to create concrete evidence in his favor that you are a Crazy Stalker and he is The Victim. His manufactured precursor to this was his blatant disregard for your humanness (devalue and discard) and the ultimate creation of an emotionally charged atmosphere of drama and chaos that sent you spiraling down into frenzied emotions where you reached your ultimate breakdown...he smugly stands calm and stoic to call the police or to get a restraining order (this is the point where some will secretly record your break down to show his enablers).

He is The Calm Force; you are The Crazy. This play on opposites should be a sure sign to witnesses, the police and others in the family court system: It is NOT normal to stand back in eerie calm as your partner is in distress.

There is a powerful and pervasive dynamic that goes on between the disordered and the non-disordered during court and other legal issues: Narcissists, narcissistic clerks, lawyers and judges destroy the innocent in family court and other legal systems because they are detached from the Universal Law of Cause and Effect; they thrive in negative environments. Whereas, the non-disordered can barely breathe in courthouses and during legal matters because we are tuned into the sickness that resides in these places. Narcissists appear strong, self-assured and righteous during court and/or legal situations whereas the non-disordered look emotional, defeated, and unstable. We wrongly think that we are *bad* because we are absorbed into the bad that others create.

<u>*Taking Away Our Peaceful Living: Our Homes*</u>

Narcissists cut you off from living within humanity by turning your neighbors against you. You are filled with extreme anxiety, animosity and anger toward your neighbors not knowing the full scope of their involvement with The Narcissist that resides with you. Narcissists have an uncanny ability to create anxiety ridden environments between people in such a way that everyone is afraid to speak to each other directly; he is the main conduit for distorted information between people. You become isolated in your home because he manufactures chaos and confusion behind your curtained windows but portrays himself saint-like to the neighbors. He keeps you hiding out from your neighbors because he mastered an illusion of your *craziness*. Narcissists know that nothing in their lives is permanent and he is programmed to act in a way to end permanency. He knows *this too shall end* so he operates in a way to leave behind a 'great man' legacy wherever he lives and goes.

I lived this same humiliation and ostracization by neighbors as a young girl living in a gloomy and dying industrial town in the 1980s. My father was an unrefined and uncontrolled Sociopath, perhaps Borderline, so he did not hide behind an image and nor did he wear a mask. Sociopaths and Narcissists have evolved since my childhood...many of us have. I lived in a time and a place where The Mafia still ruled though they hid behind their Italian restaurants serving spaghetti and meatballs on red-checkered tablecloths. The backdrop was a depleted, sorrowful and dilapidated steel town with boarded up downtown areas. My father fit the setting with his crowbar and baseball bat that he brandished at the neighbors for cutting their grass over onto his shaded mower-marks. Then came The Leaf Wars in the fall. If the neighbors didn't rake the falling leaves from their trees fast enough, and the wind carried those leaves over into our yard, there would be chaos.

And then the blood-curdling screams that escaped our walls and echoed throughout my neighborhood when my father entered into one of his fit-storms. I'm sure the neighbors didn't hold anything against the children of this household, but then again, some people do hold children in judgement. Just like now, into my present, people hold onto their image of "crazy wives" living in households they know nothing about.

I bought a home because I decided that Turk Narc sabotaged me for the last time. Previous to buying my new home and his TRO filing, I rented a beautiful apartment. It is my destiny to sabotage myself for love. I proudly told Turk Narc about my new home. He came over my first day in it and crumbled to the floor crying that he wanted me to live with him. He told me the landlord was a bad man that wanted to sneak in with his keys and do all sorts of horrible things to me. He proceeded to reveal fairy-tale stories of the new kitchen he was going to build: enclosed with sliding glass that opened to majestic herbal and vegetable gardens, an outdoor wood stove and skylight ceilings that revealed the stars. Within a moment, Turk Narc and I carried my unpacked boxes into his car...into my car. I was flattered that he cared so much about me that he not only carried my boxes, but my boxes were allowed in the trunk of his car. I shut and locked the door to my new apartment, mailed the keys to the landlord and lost my $2,500. A short time later, I found out Turk Narc was having sex with students at his college.

Before I discovered this, living with him was filled with stress: that feeling of being replaceable consumed me as he received constant texts from women and had strange female "friends" lingering everywhere. I realized that I would only be safe and away from destroying my own new beginnings if I actually bought, not rented, my own home. Turk Narc wanted to be my "friend" at the beginning of this process and I allowed it...I needed his 'friendship,' so I thought.

We were browsing inside a home and an obese neighbor came by to see who we were. Turk Narc despises people that are overweight and he was rude and shunned this woman cruelly. This would be the home that I bought and I had to be extra nice and accommodating to win this woman back in my favor. During my home inspection, Turk Narc asked me to go to lunch with him during this very important step and I happily ran along with him. The Home Inspector did a shoddy job and failed to report 3-walls full of mold and many roof leaks. I went to lunch with Turk Narc because I still had hope, all these years later, that he would be my soul mate (the dangers of the soul mate quest).

I discovered for certainty the sex-with-students and was grateful to find a *sanctuary* in my new home. The day I was leaving Turk Narc for good is the day he filed the TRO. Not only did he not prove I was a danger, but the judge felt it odd that he filed it on the same day that I closed escrow, and thence, he was shunned out of the courtroom. The mold emerged and I had to battle the HOA for not revealing structural defects. At the same time, I was dealing with the TRO and dwindling inside myself with the unexplained loss of my co-worker's dog while in Turk Narc's presence. I was then informed that my teaching contract would not be renewed because of "poor classroom management skills." I finally lost the teaching nightmare because of only ever gravitating toward bad classrooms and gang schools.

I needed *saving* so I flew into the arms of another man...My Sociopath. This is what led me into that Vanagon with that second controlling Turk. I allowed my mother's festering wounds to ooze inside all my bad decisions...add the two drinks and one encounter in a Vanagon and I shattered what was left of my life. I soon discovered My Sociopath made a duplicate facebook account as mine, same name, same picture, and was posing as me on the internet and writing strange things to people from my past. When I confronted him on this (or similar scary things), the whirlwind manifested. He lied, then contradicted, then blamed me and then played word-salad...taking my words, twisting them and then attacking back with a mangled mess of madness. When he exhausted all the deflection tactics, he went running from my condo, hunching himself over with arms squeezing top of head, chin forced into chest and loudly groaning. My neighbor, the same obese lady that Turk 1 shunned, could not help but notice the wounded animal in front of her window and came running to his aid. He cried in confusion that he *didn't know what was wrong with me, he didn't understand, he didn't do anything wrong at all.* I went from allowing Turk Narc to take my new apartment, to him crazy-making during the purchase of this new home, to My Sociopath flopping around outside my new home in an excruciating condition. Self-sabotaging cycles repeat in our lives: I allowed men to not only ruin me, but to destroy my homes and to steal away my safe living.

Before these episodes, My Sociopath eerily smiled and told me his ex-wife "screamed on the streets." That *things were so out-of-control with her that she would pick a fight with him and the result would be her running outside screaming.* She lived in shame in her neighborhood and could not go outside. My Sociopath told me the same story about his former live-in girlfriend; the neighbors hated her, loved him, and she too "screamed on the streets." I payed attention to these stories of exes' "screaming on the streets" so I stayed inside my condo and screamed in my head. I allowed My Sociopath to writhe and undulate in pain outside, in front of the neighbors, and all because of my *severe abuse.* I was learning to not react to his mental sickness.

To this day, I have vultures circling over my head looking for scraps. My Sociopath does repair favors for the little, old, judgmental ladies in my neighborhood. He walks into their homes with tool-bag in hand, Saint and Savior presence, weakened and hunched over with despair from my dreadfulness. I have not interacted in any way with My Sociopath for three years, the neighbors have never spoken a direct word with me and they have only seen me behave with respect, and yet, I am the carrion of the neighborhood. An elderly woman drives past my home (the opposite direction of her home and away from the exit out of our neighborhood), stops at the end of my driveway, annotates in a notebook regarding the nothingness going on and reports back to My Sociopath for more repair favors. This is done daily. At first, this irritated me. Now, I see...

Stupidity is really an illness that should be pitied and that evil is only a symptom of that stupidity. The world is densely populated with such unfortunates, stumbling through their lives in a heavy stupor **(Szepes, 104).**

FIFTEEN

THE BREAK-UP, GET BACK TOGETHER CYCLE

Long before the final discard, you left The Narcissist several times. In my case, I left both Turk Narc and My Sociopath too many times to remember. However, they pulled me back into the relationship with a mere few and simple words. I interpreted these pleads for my return as both their inner hurt and their intense love for me. I absorbed the desperation in their eyes, the softness of their voice as signs of eternal and soul-love; I saw them as wounded animals in need of caring. In a drop of a hat, with no promises of better treatment, I returned to their clutches. No questions asked on my part; no requirements set, no expectations imparted. I merely accepted their offer of a cheap lunch (literally), and I happily sat with my vegetable Pad Thai feeling a sense of sighed relief that I was back to *normalcy and old comfortableness*. I wouldn't have to be alone or go through the difficulty of meeting someone new. I wasn't processing that this normalcy and comfortableness included all the same games, lies, manipulations and betrayals beyond any well-grounded woman's forgiveness. I set all these facts aside and conveniently forgot all memories during this pattern of the same ol' lunch, with my same ol' forgiveness, in order to return to my same ol' Turk.

Perhaps you are so stressed-out and emotionally exhausted that a lunch out is a small reprieve away from Narcissist destruction...though the reprieve lunch is WITH Narcissist Destruction. An additional factor for me is that I tend to stop eating when upset (many people do the opposite). I must admit that a lunch out with my abuser is also a vacation from my self-inflicted starvation. Mostly, I've accepted lunch with my abuser just so that I can have an emotional break from my mind's incessant twirling that blames myself for everything. By reuniting with him, the burden that I carry that everything is my fault is relieved from my conscience; it's a fresh start for my mind: *If we're back together, then I might not be so bad after all.* I am having an *emotional lunch break* from the inner turmoil he creates within me. At these many Lunch Reunites, there is no clarification of his previous lies and disloyalties. I know that if I want to untangle my tired brain from the chaos he creates, I will not mention anything and just enjoy the time we are together...*It must have all been my imagination...my overreacting.* I trick myself into believing he is a new man and it is a new relationship.

Trust is rarely built once it is destroyed. After the lunch, we both move on to our *normal relationship* as if nothing ever happened: I sweep it all under the Thai Lunch Menu, put on my blinders, and the relationship built with Narcissism continues its course.

Narcissists are always pulling ex-debris out of the rubble.

The break-up, get back together cycle occurs because he hasn't found a new, primary source of ego-attention. When he finds someone new, he will disappear...no more Lunch Reunites. However, he may return and *Lunch You* again as secondary ego-source, or female "friend," when his newest ego-source becomes boring or she holds him accountable.

I made life extremely simple for Turk Narc and My Sociopath:

✔ *Do whatever you want to me*

✔ *I expect very little*

✔ *Eventually, I can't take anymore and erupt with emotions*

✔ *I leave*

✔ *You ask me to return*

✔ *I return with no standards or expectations*

THE BREAK-UP, GET BACK TOGETHER CYCLE

✔ *I am easy.*

I was in a constant state of devalue and discard as a child. I lost my tennis shoes when I was nine years old. The houses in Ohio have attic-ways with staircases, basements, crawl spaces, porches, patios and attached garages. Who knows where a child could have left her shoes? Losing my shoes sent my father into a tirade and he beat all of us, including mother. If my mother made a halfhearted attempt to stop the violence, he knocked her to the floor and slammed her head into the kitchen linoleum. Father searched for those lost shoes and I prayed they would never be found. When they were found, he tied the shoelaces together and strung them around my neck: A reminder to never lose them again. I had to keep those shoes around my neck all day, all night. I ate with the shoe necklace and was made to stay sitting at the dinner table long after everyone got up. I sat in the dimmed kitchen only illumined by the flickering TV that my father watched in the dark, adjoining family room. I'm sure he wasn't focusing on the show but thinking about the lesson the girl weighed down with shoes had to learn. I was then sent to bed to sleep with the shoes wrapped around me...soles on chest...clinging to my heart.

I still feel the weight of those shoes.

My father's tantrums lasted for days, then, all was *normal*. I don't know if he felt guilt or he came out of an altered state but he then took us all out for Chinese food (no Thai food in Ohio when I was a child). I still feel safe, settled and at home in Chinese restaurants. When Turk Narc lied or betrayed me, I sought out solace by settling my aged-soul and its attached bones into relic booths in old Chinese restaurants that were long ago ignored by those who sought out trendier places. Or, my father took us on a spontaneous four-hour drive to Niagara Falls with a quick view of whatever-spot and just as a quick turn-around back home. My mother smiled and told us *he felt bad* and *he wanted to make it up to us* and plus *our family knows how to have fun.* Father was in a state of manic happiness and energy: he *loved* us.

THE BREAK-UP, GET BACK TOGETHER CYCLE

When I became a teenager, Father's Returns to Normalcy also consisted of him giving me a credit card and allowing me to go clothes shopping. When he entered back into darkness, my image was trashed and my new clothes were taken away from me. I was forced to go to school in old clothes that no longer fit. Father found an old polyester pair of brown slacks that I wore as a child and forced me to wear them. I shook ascending the stairs of the school bus as he watched me from the top of our driveway. This is where I learned to be stoic. I was groomed to be a woman without boundaries and to tolerate any treatment.

To this day, men with manic energy mixed with emotional detachment are drawn to me as I am to them. I am now learning that this "manic energy" is not emotional attachment but of cold, detachment. The Manic Energy Guys are the ones brave enough to approach women. I never approach men so this sort of man will be the type that I end up with, when in fact, I need a librarian, researcher, philosopher or lone scientist. This brand of measured and more stable man would never approach me, he lives cautiously, and if he did, I wouldn't be interested.

Narcissists do not have surface emotions like Empaths but nonetheless, they have vulnerabilities. You leave your abuser, he begs for your return, you return, you leave, he begs...during this time, you have all the power. It does not matter his selfish motivations, he is still asking something of you and this puts him into secondary position. Narcissists do have emotions contrary to unthinking and repeated media sources...they are just more crusted over than ours. Their asking you to return is where they are the most vulnerable...once a Narcissist conquers a target he cannot handle her rejection. If you refuse to return to him, he is likely to crack emotionally open and you could penetrate his vulnerabilities and get him to behave like a responsible man. However, this will not be permanent and you will be in trouble again. He will start his usual games in a matter of days...maybe even hours. Nothing with a Narcissist is real, stable, or enduring.

THE BREAK-UP, GET BACK TOGETHER CYCLE

Each return to him and resulting honeymoon period is less intense, shorter lived and The Devalue is quicker and more cruel. Narcissists are initially intrigued by our open heart during the first honeymoon period, but each subsequent go-around, they despise this and gravitate toward winning over more elusive forces. We are too easy for him; a non-challenge to his ego. His ego needs the stimulating hunt of constantly new and challenging ego-sources and when we make ourselves too available by forgiving his cruel acts, we become insignificant and boring. His mask completely falls off after a few go-arounds and he becomes boldly and overtly abusive as opposed to manipulating and covertly abusing; he makes it apparent that we are being excluded, lied to, cast aside, replaced, neglected, and not considered. He will rub this in our face and when we cry, he jeers at us that we are being excluded because we cry...gaslighting...turning-the-tables.

The more times he gets you to return to him, the more he is emotionally distancing himself from you. He is transforming you from intimate partner into secondary ego-source. When the transformation is final, and some time has passed, he will respect you more in this position. In actuality, despite your feelings, you are not demoted but promoted. You will receive more respect as his secondary ego-source, or herd member, than as his intimate partner.

His intimate partner is living through hell-cycles and you are a few steps removed, still living through hell-cycles over being devalued, discarded, not getting closure and his quick returns to love-bomb you to only disappear, but you are now a few feet removed from the inferno, and you are able to have moments of realization and healing-flickers where you are slowly, but steadily, waking up.

Some devalued and discarded exes will go into secondary ego-source position because they are cunning enough to use The Narcissist for his random attention and love-bombing. Many narcissists are sadomasochists and they derive pleasure from both controlling and abusing (sado), and being controlled and abused (maso). Other exes will go into this position because they lack self-esteem...they sit quietly and wait to gobble up his crumbs. He always destroys those closest to him. It is uncanny how The Narcissist can thoroughly brainwash his former intimate partner to believe that he will be her great friend. There is a complete disconnect in her mental processing: The Narcissist could not be trusted with her heart but now they are "friends?" Absurd.

The more severe the personality disorder, or sociopathy, the less likely he is to manifest "friendships" out of former lovers. The more codependent and the bigger people-pleaser he is, the more likely that he has so-called female "friends."

Narcissists respect those who are emotionally and physically distanced more than those who are emotionally and physically available. They shutter and withdraw at any sense of responsibility or accountability. Narcissists prefer to give to people who are not asking for or expecting anything; and to these they will be the most generous.

Narcissists operate expertly on the superficial relationship level but cannot maintain anything or anyone of significance in their lives and they destroy good. Good threatens them. They cannot intimately bond for fear of loss of their own control. A deep, emotional bond puts a Narcissist at the mercy of someone else. No intimate partner can lose themselves enough to provide the amount of attention and adoration that he needs. He realizes this soon after the lustful and highly energized honeymoon period, and he will sabotage the person that he knows will never be able to completely sacrifice her soul over to him. He fears real intimacy, love, and commitment. His lying, not revealing, and seeking other sources of attention creates a fissure in intimacy and in true bonding and he does this in automatic pilot.

Since our society operates superficially, Narcissists can thrive in meaningless relationships where emotional connections are not required. This is why we go from a madly loved intimate partner to a secondary ego-source, or to a lunch buddy and sometimes sex-reunite partner, in a short time. When you are at your most intimate with a Narcissist, he will shock you by saying that he wants to turn you into a "friend with benefits." Narcissists hone in on superficial and damaging societal trends that serve their purpose to devalue those who love them. The Narcissist wants non-threatening, non-accountability, non-responsibility in all his relationships. He wants to stay a child: All fun and games...no real life.

A Narcissist hates himself and only feels an illusion of "like" for himself when an ego-source is adoring him and believing in his perfection. Each time we return to The Narcissist after his cruelty, he intuitively senses a dimming of our adoration, or even outright knows this by our anger toward him, and this acts to fade his charged up ego that depends upon excessive admiration. He has a severed life-thread that links personality to soul (sutratma) and as a result, he does not vibrate as soul, therefore, he does not recognize soul in others. Thus, the more chances that another soul-infused person gives to him, the greater distance he creates from that forgiving source. A Narcissist considers those who repeatedly forgive as weak forces and this reminds him of his own vulnerabilities.

We must also remember that The Narcissist is always fighting for mother's love, acceptance, and approval. He was either denied this, or it was offered to him in an unhealthy way - without controls and boundaries. Subsequently, he is not intrigued or turned on by someone that is too easy.

We keep returning to The Narcissist because we wrongly believe he developed a higher consciousness or was enlightened since our last breakup with him. We place our own attributes upon him. We think that he will finally SEE us. However, he is incapable of anything deep and meaningful and only wants superficial surface displays: flattery, ego-stroking, admiration, validation, attention... In the case of being devalued, discarded, and pulled back in at his every whim and beck and call, we must practice self-control. He is all Personality and though Personalities are fun, Soul is lasting.

A Narcissist is envious of those who have strong souls and that are not so easily impressed by his surface display. Instead of being his always available ego-pawn, be someone he envies. Work toward improving your life. If anything wakes him up, you glowing in your own world, instead upon him, will. Control the forces in your life...don't be controlled by them. Stop wearing his burden around your neck.

SIXTEEN

SUMMARY OF PART THREE: THE PLAY

The Script of The Narcissist "Shakespearean" Drama

Actors: The Narcissist Ego, Primary Ego-Source (also Discarded Ego-Source), Secondary Ego-Sources, New Primary Ego-Source

---

1. **Narcissist Ego Hunts New Target:** Hunt excites Narcissist and New Target

2. **Narcissist Ego captures New Target**

3. **Narcissist Ego and New Target experience Honeymoon Period:** Gains complete physical, emotional and mental control over her

   Narcissist is wearing mask of The Perfect Man. New Target acts to perfection as well. New Target and Narcissist are equally addicted to each other

4. **New Target is Primary Ego-Source**

5. **Narcissist Ego Hunt is Over:** He won The Challenge

   Narcissist stores Primary Ego-Source safely away; puts her on Narcissist Ego Shelf

6. **Narcissist becomes bored:** He needs stimulation; plays with Secondary Ego-Sources

Adult Children or other family members; Female "Friends;" Distant "Friends;" Neighbors; Enablers; Support Group Members

7. **Primary Ego-Source feels neglected:** Realizes she is being coldly disregarded

   Senses that he is no longer *there,* he is gone, vacant; he is a shell of the man that won her over

   She goes into shock

8. **Primary Ego-Source goes into reaction mode**

9. **Narcissist Ego cannot and will not deal with Primary Ego-Source's reactions**

   Narcissist has never taken responsibility for anything, his entire life, let alone his effects on others; he does not deal with issues

   Narcissist increases lying and starts cheating

10. **Any *feelings* Narcissist had for Primary Ego-Source are gone**

11. **Narcissist devalues Primary Ego-Source in a variety of covert and overt ways**

12. **Primary Ego-Source reacts more**

13. **Narcissist Ego Discards Primary Ego-Source:** Smears her with Secondary Ego-Sources

14. **Narcissist Ego becomes "The Victim"**

15. **Former and now Discarded Primary Ego-Source becomes "The Guilty" and "The Isolated"**

Brief Intermission

16. **Narcissist Ego Hunts for New Primary Ego-Source:** Needs to feel *alive* again

17. **Narcissist Ego finds New Primary Ego-Source**

18. Narcissist Ego soon becomes bored: There is let down or trouble with New Primary Ego-Source

19. Narcissist Ego returns to previously Discarded Ego-Source: Tries to turn her back into Recycled Primary Ego-Source or into a Secondary Ego-Source

He does Ego Check: Runs a test on previously Discarded Ego-Source to see if she still adores him.

He provokes rekindle sex or convinces her they can be good "friends."

If previously Discarded Ego-Source is Codependent she will allow herself to be re-categorized as both Recycled Primary Ego-Source Sometimes or Secondary Ego-Source Sometimes (female "friend")

More self-assured Discarded Ego-Source will either use and exploit him for his quick, love-bomb returns (his "great female friend") or else tell him to go to hell (his "crazy ex").

Cycle repeats forever for Narcissist Ego...

Narcissist Ego is trapped...he never learns, he never grows, he never evolves...he dies lost, lonely, and unfulfilled...

The End

Part Four...Healing

SEVENTEEN

TRAUMA AND STRESS

My naiveness is a defense mechanism in a cruel world: If I act like a small animal, larger animals will keep me safe. This contradicts not only the organization of nature, but of the logical running of our sociopath world of predators that use the blood of prey for their own feeding; sharks circling in waters smelling for blood.

Trauma

The Discard projects us onto a destructive path. We fall into shock because of the cruel way that we were tossed aside like trash by someone who was supposed to have loved us. It is even more alarming because no one sees him as we do. We are never validated. There is a chasm between who he is with us and who he is with them – his supporters. We start reflecting back upon the other people who hurt us. Some victims of narcissist abuse may even put themselves at risk for jail or court-time by obsessively tracking The Narcissist and his new target. Though consequences are due to all those who cause harm, by our involvement in it, we fall into the trap that The Narcissist set for us. He wins again: He is "The Victim" and we are "The Bad."

Our environment falls into chaos. Our home is no longer a home but piles of junk and debris that we can no longer sort through and organize. It is too overwhelming and our brains cannot make sense of not only our inner-frenzy but our outer-chaos. Hundreds of cards, emails, texts, pictures of the predator remain in our home and on all our tech devices because we believe that these remnants can shed clarity in the mass confusion that he convinced us was "true love." The pictures with him seem loving. When the picture was taken, we remember feeling that he was our soul mate. By keeping the remnants we think the answers will someday be found, that someday in the future these *love pictures* will be truthful again. We enter into an emotional black-hole as the Narcissist thrives in what appears to be a new, energetic, bright light. We've encountered a force, circumstances, that don't make sense.

As reality emerged and I saw the pattern of allowing myself to be absorbed by bad people, I became a deer frozen in headlights. I couldn't move and would just pace in my house not accomplishing anything. I was exhausted all day and couldn't take action. Add to this the fact that a Narcissist ruins our family and friend relationships and destroys us financially, I was left alone and in poverty; I couldn't even get to the nearby beach for a much needed break from my inner madness. I was angry at my mother for not protecting her children...for not teaching us how to be treated by other humans and for allowing us to be destroyed without the permitted ability to honor and protect ourselves. I was confused about my lost life. Where did it go? I knew the answer: My life was given over to bad men...I allowed bad men to absorb me.

I was diagnosed with Juvenile Diabetes (now called Type 1), autoimmune related...my body was worn out from the stress of fighting to survive on my own for so long. It is rare to be diagnosed with Juvenile Diabetes over 20-years-old. This is very different from Type 2 or what is known as the diet and lifestyle diabetes. I am declining insulin treatment (mandatory for Juvenile Diabetes or death is imminent) and instead treating myself with a modified paleo diet or very low carbohydrates, no sugars, and instead of all the beef and pork products, I consume primarily organic vegetables (non-starchy) mixed with some fish and eggs. I do muscle gaining exercises because muscle deteriorates quickly with this disease. I've been successful longer than medical history has ever recorded. Type 1's only survive a few months after diagnosis without insulin. I've now gone two years. We are more powerful and in control of our inner and outer healing than we imagine, but we must fight for our own survival. Narcissists can destroy us down to the cellular level. If you cannot seem to find energy again, after several weeks out of an abusive relationship, get a medical check-up.

Self-hatred consist of not only feeling disconnected from our core (passions and beliefs) but from our physical existence. Narcissist abuse is emotionally devastating but when we neglect our physical, our internal struggles get worse. When I was unhealthy, I did not feel good enough about my appearance to be happy in my outer environment so my inner-world churned with more madness. It was difficult for me to manifest change in my life because I hated my outer body. After diagnosis, I took charge of my diet and health and soon regained a better appearance that made me more comfortable presenting myself out in the world again...I had renewed hope. Working on your physical health and appearance brings a freshness to life and the feelings of endless opportunities.

It is often repeated that we must work on our insides first (emotions) and then our outside health will manifest. I believe it is the opposite: We must work on our outsides first (physical health), so that we will feel more confident and motivated to present ourselves to the world in order to strive toward more opportunities that are available out there.

Facebook Trauma

I see facebook and social media as a great detriment to not only people that need to heal, but to all people. There is so much madness in our world, why add the facebook insanity of how many "likes" received and hitting "like" to be "liked?" We, similar to the Narcissist, are seeking validation; and the more depressed and anxiety ridden we become, the more validation we seek. It is a vicious cycle.

Our soul energy is sucked away by comparing ourselves to not only others, but to The Narcissist: postings of unimportant details; strange selfies; one-second, happy-in-appearance images. This is an impediment to our growth. We spiral down into comparison thoughts when there is no comparison to a superficial image. When you choose to be absorbed by social media that is not of a higher intellectual level (good writers with good thoughts, ideas and discoveries), you are choosing to turn your back on your higher calling. Think of all the time you spend on social media. What if you applied this time to creating something new and special in your life instead?

When we visually fixate on the photo-gluttony of our Narcissist's fast-forward picture show of his *amazing, new love*, we are choosing to entwine ourselves in his sickness. We are absorbing his honeymoon and superficial representation of 'love' when it is only his low-level physical and his uncontrolled emotional body playing out his stunted mental development. We enter into the flow of his inner twisted world through social media. We are not just searching for validation and answers by watching his facebook antics but we are deliberately inflicting further Narcissist Injury upon ourselves.

We obsessively scrutinize her appearance from hair to nose to teeth to body shape. Narcissists neurotically display their new targets and their supposed new life all over social media. But nothing is new and she is no better or worse than us; she is just another replaceable people-part. This is his same manifested illness but with a different smiling mannequin. A 25, or 60 year old Narcissist acts like a 12 year old showoff all over social media.

They need to shout to the world, as their validation, that they are the good one, the loved one, the happy one, and they put on this display immediately after they shattered the previous target. This is not normal behavior and instead of his enablers hitting "like," they should use their brains to see his sickness in its eerie display.

Our own facebook addiction comes from shock and depression. We are stuck in a time warp of trying to figure *IT* out. There is a looming Narcissist Energy that continues to pull us into its twisted vortex and we succumb to its power. We are not only tired but we are self-punishing. Instead of obsessing over his momentary flash presentations, we need to unhook and realize he is on another train-wreck ride.

Obsession and insanity are closely linked and this applies to sociopaths and non-sociopaths alike.

Limit, if not eliminate, facebook and all social media unless you are a profound writer, work for a cause, are in a productive support group, or have a business.

Muscles Hold Trauma

My mother took her children on many "safe car trips." She drove to each of our schools in a car with blacked-out windows from garbage bags filled with our belongings. Hunched over from a heavy burden and with red and swollen face, my mother came into our school offices. I still remember the quietness of the little office lady entering my classroom to meekly inform my teacher that I was being removed from the school. This always seemed to come at a really great time: When Teacher was calling out each of us, across the rows, to recite out some historical date or math fact that I was supposed to have committed to memory and which I did not...I was mentally exhausted as a kid. I was saved from embarrassment again; I followed this angel lady back to the office where my mother stood waiting. My brother was already in the car so I crawled in the back seat to snuggle between the soft bags filled with clothes. Mother drove us into the next town over, Youngstown, and into the driveway of some old subdivided house. Though Youngstown was a dying steel town, my heart felt alive again...I got to start over as a new kid in a new school without the screaming house attached to my strange 6th grade image. I got to be the New Kid and though there was still a bit of uniqueness attached to children from broken homes in those days, at least I wasn't from the Broken Father anymore.

This New Life lasted one day...never two. The next day, I sat in the backseat of the car smothered by garbage bags as my mother told us we were returning to Him because I mentioned missing my friend Tracy. My father always stood waiting for us at the top of the driveway, jeans, no shirt, white belly with black hair, arms crossed casually and wearing a grin. He took charge of carrying the bags into the house and then we all climbed back into the car and went out for Chinese. I lived with this guilt for decades...just like I lived with the guilt of Monkey's death under the care of Turk Narc: *If I hadn't mentioned missing Tracy, our Run Away from Father would have been successful and I would have grown to be one of those self-assured women who knows who she is and where she is going.*

Though these "safe car trips" never resulted in my new life...to this day, I can relax and get out of my trauma-filled body when in a car.

My father screamed cutting names and insults at me when he found me standing in a sheltered bus stop with my high school sweetheart. I was 16 years old. Mark and I went for a walk on a freezing cold day and stood talking in this mini, red brick house with only three walls. Father saw us standing there and accused me of *giving Mark blow-jobs like a slut in public places;* I was *The Town Whore.* Mark and I had been together for over a year by this time, never had sex, and I didn't even technically know how to give a blow job; we were the rare young that stayed together throughout high school. I was experiencing my first love while my inner sheath and outer form was being continually attacked by hateful shouts that were shocking the cells of my emerging womanhood. My living cells were still moving forward despite the agonizing and stressful environment of their host; I was physically living but was being dismantled mentally and emotionally. I stood quiet through these insults that whirled around me like a gray and hazy mass of confusion...I was the discarded debris spinning in the eye of a tornado to only be violently dropped on the opposite side of the country.

Later, I trained myself to transcend my father's hateful words and to use sex as trauma release. Orgasms are a sheath and nervous system relief for me. However, unlike being in a car, there are negative consequences in seeking trauma relief through sex. My almost instant orgasms flatter a Narcissistic man and a love bond is built: My deep love, his honeymoon *love*. I link my quick orgasms to true love and he in return seems to love me more because I am so receptive to his great *manhood.* The Narcissist's feelings of love in the honeymoon period are wrapped around his temporary mania: his perfection, your perfection, the way you *fit* so perfectly together and the primitive thought of *our babies will be beautiful.*

(A Histrionic, Narcissistic or just savvy woman will scream way too loud and jump around way too much during sex to feed the male narcissist fake flattery...to falsely instill in him – brainwashing - that she is the best sex that he ever had when all she is doing is over dramatizing, exaggerating and behaving like a porn scene in order to stroke his ego so that she may get more "prizes" out of him. Since narcissistic men are drawn to superficial image and flattery, they are easily abused and taken advantage of.)

I fool myself into believing that I made a rare 'love' connection with a hard-core and unavailable man. I stabilized The Unstable: I penetrated his closed-off heart. I then see this man as someone who will always protect me and take away my haunts of the past. This feeds into itself and I am more emotionally connected to a bad man and have even more instant orgasmic releases. I cry when I have an orgasm with a new man because I feel that I made a healing soul-connection for the both of us. Narcissists, though aggressive, emanate soul wounds.

I don't feel physically at ease around people except when I am having sex with a man that controls me. I have a hard time making physical connections with friends, i.e., hugging and eye contact. My parents never made eye contact with me. Mother instills within me that humans are gross entities with holes that leak mucous. She lists all the human cavernous tunnels that *ooze goo*: nose junk, eye junk, anal junk, and of course, sexual reproductive junk which she never describes because that is too human, so, it is merely implied. Mother brags that she never goes *number two* as she calls it.

Mother told me that I will *bleed and need to use a pad.* I was twelve and we were sitting on man-made Mosquito Lake. That was it. She didn't even look over at me sitting on a towel next to her. I was shamed; I was going to use a pad. My karma was riding the dirty ripples of that murky lake toward my mother and into me: I was born in a town where they name their only lake after a blood-sucking and disease spreading parasite. I started my period soon after as a 6th grader in the lunch room of my elementary school. I was wearing white pants and didn't know what to do so I just sat smiling and talking as the blood flowed through my pants and upward to cover my entire backside. I pretended nothing was happening. Finally, the lunch-lady (mother of the boy that I had a crush on) pulled me out of the cafeteria and took me to the office where my mother was called. She arrived, didn't look at me, didn't say a word, handed the office worker a paper bag full of clothing and walked away. The next day the girls at school told me that I was the first one of all of us to start my period. I was mortified and claimed, "No, I cut my leg." My stomach was cramping that very same morning; I did see a trickle of blood in my pajamas from the night before and I still wore those white pants. Here is where I started living my destiny of never protecting myself and allowing myself to be damaged. Abused and neglected children start spiraling down at puberty.

When I didn't immediately fall into a regularly scheduled 28-day-cycle, mother approached me, without looking at me, and led me in front of my father so that he could ask me if I was pregnant; she disappeared from our sight. I was twelve and barely knew what a penis was and my mother was a grown woman that didn't know a twelve year old might not instantly fall into well-timed monthly menstruation. I remember feeling scared, wrong, and bad while having to respond "yes" or "no" to my having sex that resulted in "my pregnancy." Months later when I did start a regular monthly cycle, I lived in fear that something out of the ordinary would happen and I wouldn't prove myself to be good by my mother's monthly blood inspection of my underwear. She never looked at me, she never talked to me, but yet she carefully examined all my "ooze." I lived in fear that I would have a Virgin Birth.

In the pursuit of not only trying to unwind myself but to get over my fear of people and the human body, I recently entered into a massage therapy program. After massaging me, two different instructors said that my body behaves as if I suffered from a traumatic accident. I quietly went along with these same and independent diagnoses. I reside in the trauma from my past. This program taught me about sheathing. This is a layer of fascia under our skin that lies on top of muscles. In a car accident, this sheathing contracts when our neck is wildly swung around to protect us from even more trauma and injury than the typical whiplash. It relates to the cartoon image of the frozen, skeletal face of someone who died a traumatic death. My muscles are bound under my skin with tight plastic wrap and they are suffocating. I am trapped inside myself. I've had shoulder, neck and back pain since I was in college even though I always tried to be healthy and exercise. I have endless trigger points (knots) along my scapula, up my neck, and along my spine. It is a challenge for me to relax during massage: I hold on for dear life.

My frozen sheathing is exacerbated by not feeling comfortable within myself and in the world. When marching with my clarinet or baritone in the marching band of my high school, a friend told me that I stayed one-quarter of a step off from the beat of the drummer and everyone else. I fear people (except a man I mistakenly believe is my soul mate) deep down because I think they see through me to my *defectiveness* and into my insecure soul formed from being a child born into a family without love. Also, I subconsciously fear people may see the shadows of the bad relationships that follow me around or even outright hear the rumors spread by the men that own these shadows. Narcissists create and recreate bad reputations for others: The Smear-Campaign.

Being frozen inside myself and living in a constant state of stress and reaction is what led me into getting my yoga teaching certificate. Stress dissipates from my being as I step onto a yoga mat. It's another spot in the world, besides the car and being in bed with a man, that I can exhale. After I received the certificate, I took many months to practice routines on myself where I could flow my nervous system into calmness. As my specialized yoga routines worked to heal me, they worked to heal others and I realized that I was no longer a scared being afraid of touching. Because of the massage classes, I was able to do adjustments on yoga students and even started doing Thai Massage and Stretch. I feel at *home* teaching yoga and I finally realized that I am not *Bad*.

Doing is healing. Creative imagination is imperative to a healing and expanding soul.

Surpassing obstacles and childhood brainwashing is how we grow and heal. Instead of changing who you are, or squashing your healing nature, or letting others destroy your heart and recoiling inward as a result, take power over your energy by harnessing it and using it outward instead of relinquishing control and allowing others to steal it away from you.

<u>Releasing Trauma Out Of The Body</u>

◆ **Walking.** Best trauma release exercise. Combine this with deep belly expansion inhales and belly contracting exhales and create walking meditations. Lift your inhales up into your expanded chest and lower your exhales down from your chest into your deflated belly. Send positive thoughts and wishes out with the exhale.

- **Resistance bands and machines with cables.** This is muscle gaining as well as stretching and elongation to keep body limber, elongated and relaxed.

- **Restorative Yoga.** Typical and overdone warrior and down dog poses can increase body stress (foot pointing one way, head another, spine and hips yet a different way; wrist strain) and these should be minimized or avoided. The focus should be on seated spinal flexion and extension with other soft, rolling movement work done down on the mat.

- **Swiss Ball.** Trauma can be released by bouncing gently up and down, swaying side to side and pelvic tilting front to back. This loosens the hips and pelvic region and sends bound up energy resonating upward and outward, capturing and releasing toxic energy along the way. The focus on pelvic and hip-tilting and swaying releases the lower, stored up energy in the base, sacral and solar plexus as well as promoting a lightness in everyday movement. I became a great dancer because of the Swiss ball whereas before, I was deaf to the rhythms of the earth.

- **Massage.** If money is an issue, massage schools, Groupon and LivingSocial offer great rates.

- **Sun for healing.** Direct sun with no chemical sunscreens, sunglasses or hat. Twenty-minutes daily, or as often as possible, is all that is needed and if you have a light complexion, work up to this slowly. Sit with your back to the sun and read, look at paperwork, bond with pets, meditate or do work in the yard. Expose your feet and ankles and knees if can. Then sit or stand for a few minutes with your eyes softly closed but with the warmth and brightness of the sun radiating through your lids. This will improve your vision. Many people who are traumatized have poor eyesight...it's as if we are psychologically dimming our vision to the world and its reality.

◆ **Return to Nature.** Stroll in the park or nature hikes. Pull the weeds or use natural ingredients to control overgrowth instead of using chemicals that harm the environment. When you do gardening, you are bonding with the earth and it instills a sense of calm into the nervous system. Plant food instead of ornamental plants.

◆ **Food.** Take in healthy and nutritious foods. Limit eating to 2-3 times a day with little to no snacking. The less we eat the more healing time our body has. (The more you run a car, the more it breaks down.)

◆ *Sleep Much.*

The YMCA offers financial aid and has both individual and family programs for health and well-being. **Meetup** has healing groups and healthy activities at no cost.

Children who are raised in abusive homes and adults in stressful environments physically deteriorate at an accelerated rate. Our weakened physical condition feeds into mental health issues. Medical doctors (not just psychologists) need to be holistic and consider stress factors such as abuse when presented with physical bodies that are ill at ease and/or chronically unhealthy.

There is a fallow stage in our lives before we are consciously aware of our patterns and before we see, realize and harness our own light for our own growth. This fallow period is one of stagnation, low energy, sickness, sorrow, fear, regrets and of learnings and realizations of the work that we know needs to be done. This is a normal cycle in life. It is our dormancy...the slow death of our former selves, the planting of seeds for another life that will harvest and the patient waiting for the emergence of our new selves into bloom. We are rejuvenating.

TRAUMA AND STRESS

After we emerge anew, we will still be afflicted with cringing flashback moments of our former selves and what we endured and tolerated. These are flashes of a former time, another place, another dimension. These thoughts need to be embraced as reminders of how far we've traveled and used to energize our determination to go forward into a new and better cycle. I often read about the "seven year cycles" of our lives...that we experience different lives every seven years within our one lifetime. Start your new seven years now.

EIGHTEEN

MENTAL AND EMOTIONAL HEALING

Does anyone ever recover from trauma? Does anyone ever recover from narcissist abuse? Through my travels, I've talked to many victims of abuse, whether in childhood or later in life, and I have never heard of a recovery story. We are advised to seek counseling, do yoga, meditate, pray, and yet we are all still weakened and cry inwardly when flashes of how The Narcissist betrayed us enter our thoughts. So many of us struggle with insecurities, anxiety, self-hatred, repeated and destructive patterns, attracting abusive or controlling intimate relationships; playing the same record of our innate badness over and over in our head. We put our children and pets in jeopardy to find the love and acceptance we so desperately seek; we take bad jobs to save the world and to save bad people. All because we are instinctively driven to stop the cycle of evil; we are trying to heal our parents, our childhood, ourselves.

Counseling offers temporary relief. It is stress relieving and validation. We are able to exhale the wave of our despair and anxiety out into the vast ocean where it rides away, but just as quickly as we inhale, that same wave returns to crash into shore. We get an immediate sense of relief, but this is only for a moment in time and we continue to make our way in this world with internal ingredients of pain and shame. We feel like aliens stumbling out in a world of people that seem to be "okay." It is alarming how many adults tell me they've been seeing a therapist most of their life and yet, they express stories of trauma and pain. It seems we never really get over *IT*, no matter what prescription drug or counseling session we are assigned.

The Psychologist Or Counselor Must Be Considered

Many people that go into the mental health field have their own issues to resolve and this is what attracts them into this profession to begin with: to seek their own healing. A "normal" person, with a "normal" childhood, couldn't be in a line of work where dysfunction surrounds them all day. When I was a special education teacher, those around me who came from healthier families, could not believe that I taught in a crazy classroom all day. I was there to give to the young what I never received from adults when I was their age.

In addition, the psychologist or counselor is able to move us back out into the world, without proven success, without accountability and after making excessive money. We place our failure to thrive back into what we already believe to be our own *defective* hands. Real victims are easy to deal with in counseling situations because we are more yielding to help, but our yielding nature is what gets us entwined in unhealthy relationships to begin with. As a result, we are the most vulnerable to fall into ineffectual counseling situations. Again, as a teacher, if my students didn't show improvement, I was held accountable even though their home environment was the main factor and I earned a fraction of the psychologist's income.

Finally, most people that work in the mental health field have not experienced a Narcissist relationship firsthand and can be drawn into The Narcissist's psychological play and manipulation. The inner psychological dynamics involved cannot be understood by reading a textbook. If a Narcissist does show up for counseling, usually because of an ultimatum given by someone that he wants to control, he will effectively spin real situations and his damaging behaviors into opposites and appear like the victim, and even recruit the psychologist into being a supporter/enabler. He will love-bomb the psychologist. Not all "love-bombing" includes sex. Love-bombing can include flattery, appearing excessively attentive, submissive and pliable to the advice of another. If a real victim shows up for counseling, she usually has a hard time expressing her pain and confusion – the narcissistic love-bombing, devaluing, discarding, gaslighting, triangulating, smearing is almost impossible to put in words - and even if she can explain this psychological crazy-making, the counselor has difficulty in comprehending the severity of her psychological damage. In addition, the victim is not as personable, does not attempt to win over the psychologist and because of her stress, anxiety and depression may even appear "unlikable" in nature. Many psychologists, with ego issues, will be more drawn into The Narcissist than to the real victim.

With much effort and a real fear for my life, I worked through protocol and got a counseling appointment for My Sociopath. I effectively explained to the psychologist his dangerous behaviors. My Sociopath STILL managed to flip the entire session around by convincing the psychologist he was there because I didn't give him enough sex.

Mr. Oh told me that when he was given an ultimatum to see a psychologist by his fourth wife, that he talked her out of seeing anyone that didn't agree with him or like him the best; that he and his wife went through four psychologists until he settled into the one that seemed to respond to his "story" instead of the wife's version. To this day, four wives later, twenty some girlfriends later, Mr. Oh is still going to this same psychologist and receiving validation that he is the "victim" of "everyone." I sent this psychologist a nice email explaining Mr. Oh's patterns relating to Narcissistic Personality Disorder, and she blocked me. This psychologist advertises herself as an Empath abused in childhood with a specialization in the counseling of those similar to herself. She may indeed be an Empath Psychologist that still gets love-bombed by The Narcissist's "I'm A Poor Victim" story, or she is a Narcissist herself. Many Narcissists believe they are Empaths (it is important that empaths look at themselves honestly).

There is no way that a book can teach the psychological torment that we endured that results in our mental dismantling in areas such as love, bonding, loyalty and trust and the subsequent rewiring of our brain that implanted a twisted, high-stressed, roller-coaster of synapses that now fire from a ghostly-structure of tricks, trips, flips, tosses and turns down to the depths where our soul resides.

Self-Esteem Through Creative Expression

Besides talk therapy, there needs to be courses on self-esteem building through goal-setting toward creative expression. If a solid sense-of-self was not built as a core foundation in childhood, it cannot be built through thinking, reading and talking about positive thoughts. The only way to prosper in our lifetime is to build that core foundation in a form outside ourselves. From there, this outer creation becomes our positive sense-of-self. This can be anything from creating a peaceful and loving home, to journaling deep thoughts, to being a great friend or leader, to building an artistic expression in form (book, painting, song/poem, architectural structure, dance/flow routine, volunteer group, environmental/animal work).

Narcissists have no inner-self or solid foundation of individuality so they compensate for this void by feeding off of others.

The manifestation of creative expression can help some personality disordered but they have to be identified when they show up in counseling sessions and court-related matters. Art, music, painting, sculpturing, dance, singing, photography and other creative classes can lead the character disturbed toward more inner focus and a meditative and contemplative condition of calming introspection. Adult coloring classes are now popular and the many calming and healing benefits are being recognized. Mental health workers and court officials must be diligent and understand when someone with a personality disorder is playing the victim and appoint these individuals to mandated therapy where soul-expression, directed toward the arts, is one of the goals. (The above would benefit prisoners as well.)

There are ways to determine the authentic and genuine victim from the victim presenter:

The abuser has a path laid out behind him of stressed-out and so-called "crazy" people; he is surrounded by high and messy piles of emotionally reactive and dismantled people. He is always the "victim" and focuses on external sources for his troubles. His life is filled with numerous crazy-making situations and multiple failed or never completed endeavors. There are no signs of inner-reflecting or owning responsibility; no desperation to change or to heal. He has an excuse for everything.

An abuser does not sink into any negative physical, emotional, or mental after-effects as the result of his alleged detrimental life situation or relationship.

A real victim is filled with dread about the time wasted in the clutches of bad people and wants to heal. She uses introspection to try to break from abusive, tiring and painful cycles in her life – and is discouraged with the delays in her healing and what seems, to her, an overwhelming task for better emotional, mental, and physical health. She carries more burden than her share and appears frazzled, high-strung, and/or fatigued.

Ways To Quickly Spot A Narcissist

1. **More than a few exes and/or marriages:** Constantly seeking love and sexual relationships but can never make any relationship work for long-term.

2. **More than a few bad breakups:** Exes that hate him or were moved into the emotionally codependent position (extremes - no moderation in relationships based upon mutual giving and receiving).

3. **On again/off again relationships:** This applies with intimate partners and children.

4. **Lacks Focus:** Inability to stay committed to anything but runs from one person or activity to the next. Does not complete tasks;

can't keep jobs or finish education programs and seldom engages in higher-learning (excuses for not completing things).

5. **Can't be alone:** Questions to ask: Do you eat alone? If so, do you enjoy it? Have you ever lived on your own? Have you ever taken a trip by yourself? What is the longest time you've spent NOT in a relationship?

6. **Financial Problems:** Though working, cannot manage money; financial chaos. This indicates lack of impulse control and seeking stimulation through buying people, objects and activities.

7. **Addictions:** People, sex, alcohol, drugs, food, gambling, shopping.

8. ***Never uses "I" with regard to taking responsibility.***

Recovering from abuse requires purging yourself by engaging in a creative outlet and activity, or taking what is crying inside of you and placing it upon a platform to be viewed by all. We live in a time where this is accepted and creative expression that cries pain is honored and related to by many. Much of the creative arts of previous ages emanated from pain. It is often the case that the most damaged people will be the ones that create the most beautiful and explosive truths behind the creative arts and for many of us to survive this lifetime, we must tap into this spirit and create. Artists idealize their suffering so that others may benefit; they release their wounds so that we do not have to ache in darkened silence.

Broken people bring their soul forth to enact positive change on this earth:

1. **Set a Goal:** Determine what Inspires you. It is already present in your life. It is what you think and read about, talk about, teach others about...what you do when you have time, what you watch on TV, what you search for on the internet. It may not be where your degrees, certificates or job experiences are.

2. **Expand on this Goal:** Bring your goal to a form expression and infuse it with quality.

3. **Bring Life to the Goal:** Present it with an Impact!

The steps above require one-pointedness. This focus keeps us from low-level emotional thoughts (brain ramblings: fear, betrayal, regret) regarding the abuse and brings us into a higher mental plane where we are connecting our mind consciousness to soul. As a result, higher thoughts and concepts are able to form such as seeing the "big picture" in your life and understanding that this bad experience is your moving through a *passageway.*

The more you work, although at first you may feel forced, bored and mechanical, the more creative flow and inspiration will come. You will then be driven by spirit. You've already experienced many of these moments of intense focus where you were infused with higher-spirit but they came at times of extreme despair or euphoria. Our job is to infuse this creative spirit in our everyday lives and more consistently. This is done by being measured, strong, and enduring. The Narcissist is Fleeting; The Abused is Depleted. The key to growth is consistent effort and to proceed in moderation.

Sow a thought and reap an action; sow an action and reap a habit; sow a habit and reap character; sow character and reap destiny **(William Makepeace Thackeray).**

Abuse and trauma victims need outlets for expression. This does not always mean just seeing a professional in the mental health field. When I first realized that my life was a trail of narcissists, I created a Meetup group for those suffering from socio/narc abuse. There were forty members and we met at regular intervals, indoors and outdoors, and vented with each other for hours at no cost. Support-groups for domestic abuse victims are now more commonplace and are found on the internet. No one understands narcissist abuse more than someone who experienced it. This abuse is isolating because it is an invisible twisting of our brain, mind and soul. We see a world that should never exist.

Focus Or One-Pointedness

The key to my healing program is staying on track or one-pointedness. Focus on everything you do from the mundane to the challenging. Do not multitask! Do one thing at a time to the best of your ability until it is time to move on to the next task or activity. This practice is soothing and meditating and can exalt a person from emotionalism to spirit-infusion. You become the centerpiece of the creation whether this be a clean home, a journal entry, a relationship, or an art piece.

I realized that every dominant trait of a Narcissist links back to his inability to focus or adhere to one task at a time. I developed this thought further and came to an understanding that nothing ever evolves from distraction but yet everything evolves from one-pointedness:

- **Narcissist = No Focus = De-Evolution.**

- **Non-Narcissist = Focus = Evolution.**

A key to healing from trauma is to evolve and this is accomplished by doing and being the opposite of a Narcissist. I apply the following as part of my healing program:

Be The Opposite Of A Narcissist For Growth

1. **Quickly Changes Plans:** Late for commitments if a new and exciting target or activity presents itself.

   Be Consistent, Reliable, Dependable & Timely. Be true to your words and commitments. Show people they matter.

2. **Multitasking:** Not accomplishing anything important. Many multitasking efforts are toward over-stimulating senses and obtaining human attention, e.g., listening to music with headphones on while on nature hike with partner.

It is impossible to focus on two things at once. Focus on one task at a time. This will center you, calm your nervous system and send you into a state of meditation; you can even meditate while doing the dishes.

3. **Distractions:** Constantly texting and on social media while in the company of others, while driving and at work.

   Be polite and free of distractions when you are with other people...you will be appreciated and differentiated in today's insane and sociopathic world. In addition, you will be safer while driving and more productive at work.

4. **Human-Object Jumping:** People-part recycling; human-attention seeking; entourage building. All to avoid self.

   Be discerning in the company you keep. Another person will either bring you closer to or further from your dreams.

5. **No Discerning Quality:** Excessive number of relationships and frivolous activities.

   Practice Discerning Quality in people, places, food, art, books, social networking and the media. Everything infuses you with good or bad energy. For example, some places energize you and other places deplete you. Some foods vitalize you and other foods make you sick.

6. **No Going Inward:** Cannot inner-reflect regarding someone they hurt or disappointed. Cannot improve.

   Pay attention to your part in everything that goes on in your environment: Good or Bad. Adjust accordingly.

7. **Quick, Hasty and Careless:** Breaks things and makes a lot of mistakes at jobs, tasks, and with people.

Be methodical in your work and activities. Think through the details of what you are doing. This focus will create calming energy, allow you to avoid mistakes, and your life will become more organized.

With relationships, take things slowly and develop a friendship with the person first. It takes anywhere from 6-months to 1+ year to see most anyone in real action (not honeymoon or trying-to-impress action). However, this time may be severely shortened when getting to know someone with a personality disorder; you will get red flags early on in the relationship. Don't give this person the benefit-of-the-doubt because it is a new relationship and you desperately want it to work out.

You can change your life through Reflection. Thinking and being conscious of your effects upon your environment develops a sense of quality in your actions and interactions. Through the practice of conscious and focused living, worthy characteristics unfold. Be an Observer in your Field.

Narcissism: It's Primal

No Productive Control of Energy: Seeks constant *fresh* sources of stimulation and is highly energized running from human-object to human-object, activity to activity, but does not accomplish anything, and never evolves or learns from activities and the many people recycled through.

We are all driven by energies that fill our body. This energy is unrecognized and uncontrolled in a Narcissist causing it to become permanently settled in his three lower energy centers: Root, Sacral, and Solar Plexus. When this energy is not harnessed and used for a higher good, it stays low and undeveloped thereby promoting the animal or primal-energy...the hunger for control, dominance and sexual stimulation. This urge results in seeking physical pleasures, selfish satisfactions and instant gratifications.

Non-sociopaths, who can grow and expand, are more capable of moving this lower, primal, sexual energy into their heart center and thereby tapping into a love or connection energy. This heart energy can then be moved up into the throat to express creativity through healthy relationships, activities, and other positive formations. However, one must first be grounded in order to move this lower, sacral energy into the heart and throat. Grounding requires a strong sense-of-self, the ability to be independent and to direct one's own growth, and the sense to navigate our personal and unique life's path.

Today is The Day of Opportunity. What are you doing today?

◆ Recognize Your Plan

◆ Define Your Plan

◆ Become aware of your unique creative abilities to bring Your Plan to form or expression

◆ Make the necessary sacrifices

◆ Find the best way to radiate it outward

NINETEEN

OUR SOUL MATE

There are hundreds, perhaps thousands, of books on finding your soul mate and yet how many people do you know that are with their twin-half?

When we break up with a Narcissist, or when he does the final discard even though we were the one that kept leaving and returning, we fall into an inner abyss of loneliness and shock. Narcissist encounters are shocking to our system because we have no ability to comprehend that there are people who do not purely love or bond with the deep rooted sense of loyalty and devotion. We then enter a fantasy zone of thinking that he was somehow our soul mate (I'm now seeing the term *Twin Flame – meaning a supposed soul mate relationship with a lot of turmoil*) and his devastating actions were all accidental mis-alignments between our two souls. We then enter a thought process of: *If I didn't mention that to him; I shouldn't have reacted to that; If I only let him do whatever he wanted; I should have turned a blind eye; If only I were better looking or thinner; If I could have kept the honeymoon period going; If he returns, I'll be good and keep my mouth shut.*...This unhealthy and uncontrolled spiraling down of thinking takes over our brain and body; we are frozen in a mind-bending thought process of *Everything Was My Fault*. He conditioned us to believe we're at fault for everything...that we are bad, inferior, defective, wrong.

The soul mate myth (as well as *twin flame*) is a dangerous societal message cast on us: Our soul mate is out there somewhere; our other-half is waiting. The Narcissist acts like our soul mate in the beginning and thus, our soul is absorbed into his projected dream illusion. Long after he proves to be detrimental, we continue to fight to make him our soul mate. This is emotionally driven and is not based in logic. A Narcissist relationship is one of emotions: He is emotionally driven by an illusion that we will complete his emptiness and forever feed his ego, and we are emotionally driven that he is our one, true love that will always cherish and protect us and make us happy. Emotions come and go but solid and constructive relationship skills are real and endure through hard times. Effective communication, trust and loyalty are the most important traits in a healthy relationship and these attributes are not present in a relationship with a Narcissist. When we emotionally fight to keep him as our soul mate, we are keeping ourselves trapped in danger and instability. When we need him the most, he will always let us down.

We should not entwine with someone on a purely emotional level. Logic needs to be used to determine if this person is trustworthy, committed, stable, enduring, loyal and can effectively communicate through challenging times.

We emotionally obsess over reenacting the honeymoon period he played out in the beginning of our relationship, because back then, he was perfect and met all our dreams and expectations. We want this person back though this person never existed. We were sold the Knight in Shining Armor fantasy and we fell for it, and now we wish for a time-machine to take us back to a time and place that never existed. We were showered with love, attention and material items and this was not only exhilarating, intoxicating, but it was a relief to our tired souls. It is too hard to accept that we were duped; that we are no longer going to be doted on so we rationalize that perhaps it wasn't a duping at all...maybe he really is our savior but we somehow knocked him off his gallant ride...*we can return things to how they used to be.* The extreme honeymoon high and its memories are playing out as an addiction in our brain...just like thoughts of heroin to an addict. We want the *Honeymoon High* back. This was when our lives were perfect and we had hope for the future.

On another level, every human wants to feel deeply connected to another human, someone that understands and accepts every cell in our body; we even hope to find a "mind reader" or someone that can foresee all our wants, needs, and desires before we express them. Yet, it is difficult to achieve an enduring and perfect connection with anyone - even a somewhat *normal person.* Why is this? Because NO ONE, not even our one supposed soul mate, can ceaselessly connect to our daily, hourly, minute-by-minute emotional bursts of joys, despairs, needs, hopes, fears, doubts, inspirations...No one lived within us when we were children and absorbing the world that was opening up around us for our discoveries that included triumphs and traumas...the synthesizing, or the blending of lessons that were presented to us, and when we were shaping our understandings and forming ourselves into our current being. No other person can be succinctly in-line and in-harmony at all times to our internal thought processes of how we perceive the world and how we position ourselves in it as our manifested personality.

We all live within one great cosmos but yet we are all contained within our own separate universe. We cannot live within someone's universe and nor can they reside in ours. We, in essence, will always be lone creatures and will not be able to complete ourselves through another person. We must evolve on our own. We must be our own soul mate. Our completion comes from loving all life unconditionally and doing service work with no expectation of receiving admiration or accolades in return; an evolution of the expansion of ourselves and a development of soul consciousness that Narcissists are incapable of. Narcissists may do "service work" but it is not done from a ray of unconditional love and heart-wish to aid in the service of creating a better world. It is done to gain supporters, to win approval, to look good, and to find another target.

Love for humanity can include the damaged, disconnected, and lost soul of The Narcissist, but it does not mean to become entwined with his dangerous personality. What I speak of here (unconditional love toward all humanity even the personalities detached from soul) may not be developed until we see and understand the big picture. The big picture being that we are all brothers and sisters on different steps of our evolutionary path and we are all seeking healing and yearning for love. It is dreadful that Narcissists cannot find their own path and instead, tread upon the path of others to subdue their inner frenzy of loneliness.

There is no such thing as one perfect *soul mate* and the only way we can heal this perpetually unmet craving is to be our own soul mate. According to Kabbalah, "Be thyself." This means to live your passions and do the activities that you love and you will eventually find yourself and then someone with the same passions. You're more likely to meet another great soul among like-minded people with similar pursuits. Kabbalah states that this is a high-level soul connection of the *ruach* nature of the soul. It is low-level, or *nefesh*, when the attraction is on the superficial appearance level only. In the latter case, you are merely responding to the person's physical presence and how they reflect back upon you to make you feel good about yourself through their superficial attention. You, in turn, reflect back upon their superficial attention and you both become entwined in a low-level play of wrong thinking about what love is. Personality attractions do not endure real life unless a higher-level bond is developed.

Loving soul to soul is the key. This does not necessarily mean that every soul is our soul mate. We should see soul, love soul from our higher consciousness, and realize that soul mates are found through soul work. This may not include sex, passion, or the lustful honeymoon high.

Empaths are especially susceptible to instantly connecting with people to whom they think are authentic, and will fall into their own personality tendencies of immediately revealing the contents of their soul to almost anyone. We mistakenly believe all people are heart-driven and when we run across someone who seems to like us, we simply open our heart to them and want to love. Empaths are led by their *ruach* nature...we have a high and uncontrolled level of unconditional love that radiates outward, but this is not always safe for us. We must learn to be careful about making instant and deep connections with most anyone that comes along.

Predators love me, and even if a person is not a predator, they become one around me.

A Narcissist makes the instant and low-level *nefesh* connection, and it is done from his damaged soul which is driven from intense boredom and a desperate need to gain adoration, and to absorb the life-energy from others. He is a void. Many people get caught up in this *nefesh* connection and hence, The Narcissist never seems to run out of targets and supporters.

In order to heal, we must move past the obsession to find a soul mate or the despair we feel in that we lost our one true soul mate. In actuality, we may meet fifteen or more soul mates in our lifetime, and these are people and animals that offer us learning lessons and stepping stones to our higher-selves. Even The Narcissist taught us lessons that aided in our growth and awareness. If it were not for the adversities that destructive forces brought into my life, I would not be here now, doing this. I would have stayed asleep. The Narcissist was our soul mate because he brought us one step closer to our soul work. He is just not the soul mate we imagined. He is not to be clung onto but released for growth.

TWENTY

BACK TO TURKEY FOR THE ANIMALS

Open people have to travel; we have an inner drive to see the world and to absorb cultural energies. We are constantly expanding our experiences, minds and knowledge. As Turk Narc and I walked the slanted streets of Istanbul all those years ago, I felt trauma in my heart because I couldn't help the street animals. My first visit to Turkey was shocking: I could not comprehend that suffering was not only allowed, but considered normal. In these situations, Empaths doubt their perceptions, blame themselves for being "too sensitive" and force themselves to turn Apathetic to fit into the world of People; we shut down our heart and sensitivities.

Turk Narc and My Sociopath grew up on these same streets and the horror was even worse back then. It is something to consider: Does growing up in an Apathetic Country where suffering is not only ignored, but accepted, make more Narcissists and Sociopaths? I know the United States has many horrors, and a terrible pet overpopulation problem, but in most cases, homeless and suffering animals are hidden away from the view of our developing and/or sensitive minds. We do not spend our lives walking over and around the suffering. (Empaths are still tuned into and haunted by what goes on in animal shelters though we may not be literally viewing an animal shelter.) Turk Narc is cold, complacent, hardened and tuned-out to suffering, whereas My Sociopath has haunted images that twinge his bones with horrified hatred.

My Sociopath said things from his soul that indicated he never adapted to the Turkish animal horrors; he bled from his soul. His eyes grimaced and his jaw clenched as he remembered *Feast of Sacrifice*: A sheep was tied up in his childhood backyard for several days and on the appointed day where a sacrifice was to be made to Abraham, his father killed the screaming sheep and a celebratory day of a big feast ensued. However, it wasn't only this one animal screaming, in one backyard, it was the screaming of the sheep throughout Istanbul. My Sociopath ran crying through the streets, hands cupped over his ears to block out the screams. This event alone indicates the illness of a culture that raises its children, its future citizens, to not only be exposed to trauma sounds and visions, but to be removed from compassion. This screaming, the visible suffering, settled in the nervous system of My Sociopath and Turk Narc. This reminds me of 4-H in the US. Children taking care of farm animals to be later entrenched in slaughter as their "great learning lesson." I wonder how many Apaths, Narcissists or Sociopaths emerge from that?

Desensitization of children does not lead to the evolution of our species.

Sensitivity and compassion is rationalized out of the young by organized groups and religion in that it is okay to sacrifice and slaughter animals for human need, tradition and rituals. Yet, this view of animals does not negate the fact that animals feel pain, sadness, stress and are in a state of horror during their lifetime of mistreatment. Why can't countries be ruled by a dogma that man should be kind and compassionate toward the animals because they too suffer? I visited Finland, the home of my ancestors, and there was not one stray animal to be seen and there were no shelters full of animals being euthanized. I know of no Screaming Lamb day in Finland and yet the Finns are the most intellectually advanced and gentlest people in the world.

My Sociopath and I took another trip to Turkey on a mission to do something, anything, for the suffering street animals. We arrived in Istanbul and settled into his mother's vacant apartment. The trip took 2-days and I was exhausted. My Sociopath immediately locked the door from the inside and put the key into his pocket. With slithering eye slits, he pulled out a recording device and said, "I've been recording you all along and you will now listen to yourself." Long before our trip to Turkey, he was setting me up for emotional reactions, activating a hidden recording device, maintaining silence and even consoling me as I cried out in terror. I was now locked inside an Istanbul apartment and cornered by a Turkish Ghazi with an MP3 player. Horrified, I knocked the device out of his hand. It fell to his mother's hardwood floor and made a small, barely noticeable mark. He violently screamed at me for destroying his mother's apartment and lunged at me. I ran to a window and called from the 3rd story for help. Women came to their windows from the apartments across the way and stood staring at me; men walking on the streets below waved their hands dismissively up at me to say that I was an annoyance. I ran into a bedroom and locked myself in.

My Sociopath called his sister over and calmly informed her that I was violent, broke his MP3 player and I was trashing the mother's apartment; he showed her the device and floor mark to prove it. I emerged from the locked bedroom and begged the sister for help through stuttering words...my mind twisted in a knot: I really did scream on those recordings, I really did knock the recording device out of his hand and it really did make a mark on the mother's floor....but....but...I couldn't explain a force that I didn't know existed. My brain was a mess and I was 10,000 miles away from home locked in an Istanbul apartment. The sister stared at me with blankness and left. I returned to the bedroom and locked myself in for two days only to emerge when I heard Sociopath snores. I spent my locked-in time staring out from my bedroom's little balcony over to the adjacent balcony with its hanging clothes - wondering if anyone was happy over there - and why do I not only accept bad men, but stay with bad men. I finally came out of the bedroom with a smile on my face to please My Sociopath and a Will to help the suffering street animals.

All those years ago I submissively followed the manic strut of Turk Narc over and around the suffering animals and now I knew, no matter what, I was going to stay in Turkey with a bad man to help the animals. Not all soul mates dance around us with flowery love...some put us in extraordinary situations so that our own soul can lead the way. I had to return to Turkey and it was going to be with My Sociopath: I was on a mission...no matter what.

WILL does not require forced energy and effort. Will is what makes you: what you think about, gravitate toward, and what you do when given a chance.

We spent over a month in Turkey. I led up a trap, spay-neuter, re-release program for the starving street cats and dogs. I worked endless hours connecting to various British animal-rescue groups to obtain humane traps, and to establish contacts with Turkish vets that would take the US dollar bribe to spay-neuter the trapped street animals. I had to instruct and motivate local Turks in the follow-up maintenance, or feeding and providing basic care for the animals once altered and re-released, and how to use the traps and vets to continue the project once I was gone. I studied Turkish for a year before this trip and brought the program to study on my laptop while in Turkey. My Sociopath hid my laptop and I could not continue my learnings. However, I talked as much Turkish as I could and received Turkish smiles and laughs in return. My Sociopath stood there, vacant, for the entire month, and asked me to take pictures of him standing amongst the mass array of humane traps and street cats coming out for their feeding. He used these same pictures and my rescue project to capture his next target...she is a Turkish animal lover.

My Sociopath had an entourage of visitors from his old days in Turkey and a visitor that flew in from the United States. He made me cook and clean constantly to entertain them between my hours of animal-rescue work. The calm, beautiful and warm Aegean waters rippled within feet from where I was working and yet, I stepped into these waters one time. My Sociopath played the ultimate game of divide and rule between everyone. He regularly complained to me how horrible one of these visitors was and told me of his plans to abandon this person on the streets of Turkey. I consoled My Sociopath while still defending this other person and making sure he wasn't dropped off and abandoned. All along, My Sociopath whispered to me that this person didn't like me, and to this person he whispered that I didn't like him.

I knew that evil walked alongside me those days in Turkey but I was assured that I made a positive contribution to not only the current suffering animals, but to those innocent creatures who would be relieved from being born into hardship and then death. I also believe that I instilled good into the hearts of some Turkish people. My Sociopath allowed me to work until exhaustion because this aided his people-pleasing nature and he looked good to his neighbors in Turkey. His family has a vacation home where I did most of my hard work. He is now the hero there and all his facebook pictures show it.

Weeks later, we arrived back to Istanbul and sat at a three-tabled cafe on a narrow, crooked, tilted, side-street outside the Grand Bazaar. I bought nothing for myself the entire month in Turkey. I asked for a rice pilaf; the cost was $1.00 US. My Sociopath insisted that I share a pasta side with him. I wanted the pilaf and I stood my ground; rare for me but I was depleted. This enraged My Sociopath...he spit hatred across the table and glared the reptilian stare at me. Shivers shimmied up my spine. He called me a "pig." I ate the rice pilaf with guilt and in terror. I paid the hell-price after. He ignored me for the entire 26-hour plane trip home. I fulfilled my mission...I returned to help the animals of Turkey.

I turned down living with Professor Turk Narc all those years ago because he told me that my pets would have to live outside. I have an inner compass, a Will, that despite who is consuming me, I am driven to protect the animals. Fifteen years and another Turk later, I stayed with My Sociopath far too long but toward the end of this long cycle in my life, I returned to

Turkey to establish one of its most organized trap, spay-neuter, re-release programs to that date.

I now live on my own and am happily driven by my inner-compass but without the damaging sources in my life. I am struggling financially but I am happy to have a roof over my pets and my head, a car that drives, and food to eat. Besides my two rescue dogs, I live with a raccoon. Well, I think it's a raccoon, he or she makes a lot of racket under my house. I feed and water him/her nightly and everything is wiped clean in the morning. I think about the raccoon that bit me all those years ago with the fondest of memories and hold no grudges. I've never seen my housemate so he/she may be a large rat. It doesn't really matter because even a large rat is a more beautiful soul expression than My Sociopath. I am no longer consumed by negative forces, and I still make blunders with men, but nowhere near to the Marry or Live-In Blunder. I relish in freedom without a dark and heavy force pushing down on my spine...and if I choose to do so, I may have a side of rice pilaf...though, I should probably go on insulin first. I even, recently, sought out that Tuscany restaurant, with the cracked cement floors and thinly layered eggplant dish that I so loved, and that Turk Narc ruined for me on my birthday because he didn't want to eat food that would destroy his skin's elastin and collagen rebuilding properties...but it went out of business. I made exciting plans, in my head, to celebrate life on my own...

TWENTY-ONE

ALL MY LESSONS WRAPPED UP IN ONE

If you stop and examine your life, you will realize that you attract those people and situations that activate your wounds (childhood and relationship trauma) and send you into negative emotional reaction mode. However, if you enter inside of yourself when you are emotionally out-of-control, you will discover the key to what you need to avoid. From this point, you can learn to understand why you attract what you do and most importantly, what you need to attract instead. We need to learn about ourselves and our patterns by using our intellect to access our negative emotions and our automatic acting out of unhealthy patterns. Through the use of our brain we start creating new habits to use our energy wisely and not toward negative forces.

I wrote the above about a year ago. I am now in the process of editing. I have been trying to operate through my intellect and not allow the ruling of my emotions. However, I can still get tripped up. We must keep moving through a set of experiences that appear different, yet have the same results, until there is emotional control, mental understanding and a soul realization. Evolution is repeating cycles until you get *IT* karmically, through time or events, and only then is the cycle finished.

Mr.Oh, 65-years-old:

- Married and divorced four times

- Six children by three different women

- No one in his family achieved a higher education, including parents, former wives, all adult children and himself*

- No family member ever lived on their own, or paid their own bills or traveled on their own

- All family members, including himself, live by instant gratification and fail to obtain higher goals or even self-reliance

*Education is not just a sign of intelligence but of the ability to focus, surmount obstacles and to be loyal and committed to goals. It is Delayed Gratification which is the opposite of the Narcissistic trait of seeking Instant Gratification. Those with personality disorders live for Instant Gratification and this chaos is manifested from parent to offspring and it penetrates through generations.

I was tripped up because Mr.Oh presented himself as someone trying to evolve: a yogi, a Buddhist, a reader of philosophy, a thinker, and someone looking for love or a serious relationship in his final years of life.

Though his past was bad (to say the least), I mistakenly believed that because he was much older, he was at a redeeming stage of his life. He fit an image of my ideal...older but fit, tall (yes, shallow of me), a good thinking mind, did not drink, smoke, or do drugs, but most of all, he wasn't Turkish. My grandfather, father, brother and nephew shared his name.

Mr.Oh confused me but here is where my evolution occurred: My stumble was temporary and only a minor emotional hurt. Because of my knowledge regarding the personality disordered, I was able to keep things in perspective when I saw signs that I should not fall in love with him. Instead, I kept writing my book and then I slipped Mr. Oh into its pages. Focus and creative work is imperative to a good life filled with meaning, perspective, and mental wellness.

My evolution occurred on many levels. I realized the same man keeps showing up in my life but with vastly different presentations. I also acknowledged that because I spent three-years reading and writing about

Narcissism and Sociopathy, I saw all emotional manipulators and controllers as having one or both of these disorders. I started seeing that some people are primarily selfish, spoiled-brats, basket-cases from never receiving teaching, guidance and loving discipline from their parents and thus, refuse to see or acknowledge their lifelong pattern and its negative effects on other people. They never take responsibility, learn, grow, change, evolve. Everything is fun and games...instant gratification.

Mr.Oh is extremely self-centered but is very insecure and has low self-esteem. He has manic energy to people-please and win people over but has out-of-control emotional reactions for what he perceives as the slightest nip to his ego. Whereas My Sociopath does repair and handyman favors to keep a support group, Mr.Oh obsessively entertains people in restaurants and with stimulating activities. During the many months that I've known him, he has never spent one moment alone. All six of his adult children have no impulse control, are not responsible adults, and his chaotic personality manifests in them. Most of them are alcoholics, two have diagnosed mental illnesses and it appears that a few have personality disorders. There is always a crisis in Mr.Oh's environment and he is the one that sparks its energy.

Mr.Oh was raised in weakness and dependency and never made to take life on with his own strength. His parents enabled him to get out of Vietnam on a student deferment and then supported him when he dropped out of college. He stayed home from Vietnam to pursue one target after the next, to marry again and again, and to have baby after baby. All the while, his parents and family were triangulated in his *relationships* and she was the "bad" and he was the "victim;" he simply moved on to the next awaiting target with his parents pity that he had to escape "another bad woman." Mr. Oh had an emotionally incestuous relationship with his mother and still has this with many other family members. He now has emotionally incestuous relationships with his children...acting as their boy toy.

The Vietnam War was a tragic mistake but the energy behind Mr.Oh's family psychology to bring an Emerging Man back down into Boyhood is what is damaging, and what led to many lives being ruined here at home. Would Mr.Oh still have become a breeder and perpetual target chaser if he were forced into Vietnam and into manhood? He did not stay behind to create good at home but de-evolved into a self-serving life of irresponsibility. Evading Vietnam to be a serial breeder, serial marrier and divorcer, and all with parent support, was the dangerous impetus to him never developing a sense of responsibility, commitment, loyalty, honesty, endurance and steadfastness. This is why he creates boys and girls out of what should be men and women in not only his own adult children, but everyone he gathers around him...toxic co-dependence.

A forced activity and then a forced responsibility, relegate the bulk of those so conditioned to the nursery stage or the child state, to shoulder responsibility and its growing sense of the real values of the standards of life. The sense of responsibility is one of the first indications that the soul of the individual is awakened **(Bailey, *Education In The New Age,* 105).**

Mr.Oh creates apathy in his entourage so that he feels loved, needed and adored. He is preoccupied with turning his ex-wives and ex-girlfriends into his "best friends" and does extensive and inappropriate favors for them. He happily opens his home to any homeless and/or drug-addicted casual acquaintance that calls him begging for a place to stay – all the while cooking meals for this wayward person and immediately calling him/her his "best friend." He goes days without sleeping and when he is not with a person, he is talking with and texting people on his phone, or falling in *love* with the superficial images of women on the internet and referring to all of them as *great quality.* **He obsesses after quantity of attention and cannot discern good quality through his blurred chaos of Human Amassing.** Mr.Oh thrives off the dependency he enables in others; the same dependency that was instilled in him by his parents.

A Blurring Of Disorders

1. **Charming:** Calling or texting to see how my day was going or went; ordering for me at restaurants and coffee shops and picking up the check; opening my car door; walking on the outside when we strolled on the street.

2. **The Great Entertainer; A Creator of Events; A Love-Bomber:** Showed me the best of times: intimate jazz shows; spur of the moment acrobatic yoga lesson with him as my "flying" partner; wining/dining at quirky places along the coast; full moon meditations on dark trails overlooking the ocean; meeting me at my gym with freshly prepared food and flowers laid out in the backseat of his car.

   Insecure and low self-esteem: Driven to keep me entertained by filling our time together with constant activities; worried that I would become bored or disinterested with him. Does not feel innately loved and must keep people happy through his excessive gestures. Highly energized and creates an energy vortex around him that is stimulating for targets and supporters.

   Emotionally immature and non-discerning: Because of his high energy level, he love-bombed me and many other targets at the same time. He passed out his phone number to 45 women in ten days and was proud of this "achievement" (a grounded woman would have run at this admission; I stood frozen and was flattered to be included).

   The many targets: Non-empathetic and/or non-codependent women will quickly realize there is something wrong with him and drop out of the running.

   Women without boundaries, empaths, and codependents will be left. These are the women that fall into his trap and these are the ones that tolerate him for the longest because they ignore or excuse away all his lies, inconsistencies, stories that don't make sense, half-truths, manipulations, and lack of reliability and responsibility.

Apaths, or people that don't care much beyond survival and social connections, can also withstand him for a lengthy period. Apaths need the company of energetically charged people and will tolerate the occasional and sporadic presence of the personality disordered. An Apath needs a man around for her own identity and self-esteem, and uses him for his free meals, entertainment and excessive favors.

3. **Made Himself My Perfect Match:** Presented himself as the man of my dreams; everything I liked, he liked; everything I did, he did; everything I was, he was.

    Social Chameleon: No core-foundation, no fundamental way of being. Morphs into the person he is currently seeking adoration from. This is why Narcs/Socios/BPDs are disloyal. They are not even loyal to their own selves.

    Went to Buddhist temples with me and to a Fundamental Christian Church with a previous target.

    (My Sociopath was born and raised a Muslim Turk, turned into a Christian for the American girlfriend he left his Turkish wife for and then became a Buddhist for me. Is currently into Zionism with his current wife. Likely doesn't even know what a Zionist is.)

4. **Can't Be Alone, Can't Live Alone:** Needs constant external stimulation and adoring faces. No external stimulation to be found alone or in the quietness of his home.

    Acts like an addict: Instead of drugs or alcohol, people is the *drug* of choice. Incessantly contacts other people to meet him for coffee, lunch, shopping or to go to the gym; has to have a workout "buddy." Never goes home but drives from person to person, activity to activity.

Currently living in a 2 bedroom/1 bath, single-wide, inexpensive mobile home and has to have a roommate. I asked him if he ever lived on his own. He looked at me strangely and responded, "No, I've always had uncles and brothers that I could live with in between wives."

Would rather spend money on people-pleasing activities and cut cost on housing. Believes housing cost is an evil necessity and wants to be out wining/dining and participating in exciting activities. In reference to his home, he said, "It's only a place to sleep and shower."

Cannot vacuum his tiny home; has to call a "friend" over to help him. Will not prepare a meal or eat in his home unless someone is there with him.

Made his adult children into *Surrogate Partners* or "best friends;" has emotionally incestuous relationships with them.

Codependency develops in families where the parent does not teach children responsibility but instead teaches distractions. This creates generations of family members that cannot be alone, who lack independence and self-reliance, and who obsessively seek stimulation and instant gratification.

5. **Excessive Texting and Time Spent on the Internet:** Must constantly interact with people, anyone, to keep ego-supply abundant and fresh and to feel alive and worthy.

No quicker source of immediate stimulation.

Arrogantly claims it is all important work or family related.

After working all day with him on his manic activities and projects, I drop to bed at 1:30 am to be woken by his phone at 3 am. He does not care for my welfare (or even rights) and instead is happy that a low-quality person is calling him in the middle of the night.

6. **Late, Disorganized, Last Minute:** Rude, selfish, inconsiderate toward others.

Will be on time for work because it is a job that offers him a great deal of people stimulation, a means to receiving adoration, and the necessary money to keep targets and supporters happy.

No concept of responsibility regarding personal relationships that are already established; these people are taken for granted.

If he has plans with one target, or enabler, and another potential target, or enabler, shows up, he leaves the original person waiting.

Believes others should not make a big deal out of his rude and inconsiderate behavior and becomes defiant if someone holds him accountable.

Does not have Will when it comes to building healthy, personal relationships. Time, and its management, is under the direction of the Will, or one's innate force, to move toward a higher purpose and away from meaningless distractions.

7. **Never to Blame**: Never apologizes and never uses "I"

Never introspective. No effort to change the behaviors that lead to a life-time of the same disruptive situations. Doesn't make connections between his behaviors and the many people, and especially intimate partners, that cycle through his life.

Many situations of screaming and out-of-control wives, girlfriends, roommates, children. All exes were *bipolar or sexually neglected him.*

You will hear Socios/Narcs talking about many partners sequestering themselves to separate bedrooms long before there is an actual breakup. Classic quick honeymoon period followed by the victim realizing he is not what she thought he was. She senses danger and closes down sexually. A woman's loving emotions toward a man, and especially the sense of safety felt with him, determines her sexual response.

When I caught him with another woman in our favorite restaurant, he blamed me for *not seeing things correctly* and that he was only at this restaurant to "break things off with her" so that he could devote himself to me.

Healthy human beings stop after so many of the same bad situations, see a pattern, and try to change their own programming.

8. **Reveal a Not-so-Pleasant Truth So Everything Seems Truthful:** Done at the beginning of the relationship to create a bond.

Told me that he was dating three other women besides me. This was 6-weeks into our fiery courtship. He was "interviewing" for partners.

I was "The Chosen" (how flattering) and he was breaking it off with the others. I must be my "patient and loving-self" and wait for him (what a great person I am).

The Not-so-Pleasant Truth revealed was expertly crafted and actually made him look sexy and desirable and created a competitive drive within me to be the best; to be the winner.

My emotional processing tends to be diamond like...I don't see all the cuts and sides at once; it takes me time to flip around and notice the many facets. I wanted to be the "Good Girl."

The *Good Girl* behavior with bad men comes from growing up in a home where bad treatment had to be ignored in order to survive. If you are reading this now, you likely came from a home with one or both narcissistic parents.

We would not accept narcissistic treatment if we weren't already used to it.

9. **Financial Problems:** Impulsive and unthinking spender and shopper.

   Constantly paying the tabs of female "friends," adult children, ex-wives and supporters to gain influence, adoration, attention, and ego-supply...to be loved.

   The main target sacrifices to try to ease his financial burden. This is why she is his main target: her sacrificing ways.

   Excessive expenditures to charge-up life doldrums, or to get that high feeling, and to drown out feelings of being lost, ungrounded and detached from soul.

10. **Duping:** The prideful act of "getting one over on someone."

    Eerily laughed when he told me how great it was that he got "The sociopath writer in bed" and especially after I caught him with another woman. Laughed about how funny it was that I slept with him instead of the other men that I was dating.

    An even more extreme case of duping was told to me by an attorney. He explained how funny it was to follow his girlfriend and her husband to where they were having a meal, sit outside the restaurant within clear sight of them, and text her with her responding the entire time.

11. **Sexual Addiction:** *The Diagnostic and Statistical Manual of Psychiatric Disorders, Volume Four, describes sex addiction, under the category "Sexual Disorders Not Otherwise Specified," as "distress about a pattern of repeated sexual relationships involving a succession of lovers who are experienced by the individual only as things to be used." According to the manual, sex addiction also involves "compulsive searching for multiple partners, compulsive fixation on an unattainable partner, compulsive masturbation, compulsive love relationships and compulsive sexuality in a relationship."*

Pushed me to sexual extremes and acts. Instantly claimed me as his own and insisted we have sex immediately.

Sent me nude photos of himself without my asking and before we had sex. I never sent any of myself.

Dropped innuendos in our normal conversations, before we had sex, on how some women couldn't handle his "largeness." I was intrigued.

Obsessed with hearing me compliment his naked body.

Preoccupied with making me have orgasms. Obsessed with hearing me say how great of a lover he was and wanted to hear full details about the intensity and nature of my orgasms.

The Unattainable Sex

These women are mysterious and intriguing because they have yet to fall under his power and control; they do not adore him and are not mesmerized by him.

He is obsessed with women who do not become fully sexually absorbed within him, who do not fall under his complete sexual control, and who do not adore his *amazing* sexual prowess. He becomes preoccupied with keeping these allusive women in his life as so-called "friends." This is his attempt to keep these "friends" intrigued and foster an air of sexual flirtation between them. He hopes that someday one, or all of them, will "wake up," see what an *amazing* guy he is, and eventually change their minds and succumb to his penis. He also fears being "out of sight, out of mind." **This is his ego-battle:** he will not let go of a woman who failed to become obsessed with his allure. He keeps her around with extreme and inappropriate grand gestures that are more appropriate in romantic relationships: intimate dinners, drinks, and movies. He also wants to outshine any potential new man in her life that she may come to truly adore. He creates these inappropriate relationships with unattainable women when with a partner who has already succumbed to him and adores him (she is now easy, a non-challenge and taken for granted).

If he receives the sought-after unattainable sex, he soon becomes bored, frustrated and now holds the once mysterious woman in contempt. He turns cold, aloof and abusive to the woman because she is no longer The Unattainable. Also, she now expects truth, loyalty and responsibility after the relationship turns into a sexual one. He grows to hate her.

Narcissists make women sexually addicted to them! There is no person more powerful than a Narcissist with a large penis. They don't have to work as hard to create addictions in women; they create an instant sex-bond with a target who mistakes this low-level connection as a "love bond." Women equate a large penis with great love-making and with a powerful and strong man. This is not real love; nor is it safety and security.

12. **Perceived Insults to Ego, Circle-Talk-Hell:** Negatively reacts to typical statements or happenings that normal people can effectively navigate through.

I remarked that *his perpetually homeless female "friend" with a real estate license, who walked away from her marriage as a martyr with nothing but $500,000, and who makes him pick up all her tabs, and who he still tries to flatter in order to win her over, and who is a Fundamental Christian when he claims to be a Buddhist...doesn't make sense.*

He went out-of-control and ripped all the items from my home that he gifted to me. Ranted that I was a horrible person and threw a list at me that I hated everything and everyone. Refused to apologize for this assault.

He claimed that I hated this woman and then changed the story that he never had a reaction.

Believes he only has the most amazing quality people in his life and my remark went against this delusion.

This female "friend" was a previous "girlfriend" that refused to have sex with him. She is a User – his life is filled with Users. He is battling with his ego to get ego-supply from The User. By winning the superficial recognition of The User, his sheer sheath of "self esteem" is momentarily satiated.

Contradictory emotional and mental processing.

Cruelly attacked and punished me for pointing out a contradiction with his female "friend," yet did not defend me when a drunken woman that he associates with verbally attacked me.

More loyal to those who take advantage of him than those who are worthy and truly love him. The people who keep boundaries with him, but use and superficially flatter him, are exciting, whereas the people who give too much of themselves are forsaken.

Wants a superficial display of a silent, doting, worshiping puppet. He wants nothing real. He attracts users and toxically, codependent people who lead low-functioning lives. He can control these people and in return, these people artificially and superficially satiate his low-level ego needs for attention and validation...for a moment in time.

Abnormally sensitive to even imaginary opposition, but no sensitivity in areas where really needed; he trampled down which was most delicate in his own household (Szepes, 95).

13. **Delusional:** Most thoughts, ideas and beliefs are not grounded in reality.

    Lacks quality of discernment. Generating entourages of needy people is a numbers' game only. Fills life with Quantity not Quality.

    Believes all women he associates with are the most beautiful and the best quality. When I saw him with another woman, she appeared sickly, depleted and homeless. She drove a van with broken out windows and filled with junk that blocked the windows. When I mentioned this to him, he exclaimed she had cancer, was dying, and I was cruel to say this. I discovered he was lying. Many other exes were below average in looks and in many other areas of their lives.

Sees *beauty* in anyone that smiles at him and pumps up his ego. In actuality, he is seeing his own *beauty* in her adoration...his own reflection.

Believes he is a highly-evolved spiritual person yet possesses no attributes of a person even trying to evolve. Memorizes spiritual quotes but does not live the essence of them.

Referred to a 60 year old male co-worker as having "The whole world open to him," and has "much fun to experience with a lot of different and great women" and therefore, "he should leave his current live-in partner to pursue the prime of his life." Referred to this man as his "role model and mentor."

Immature and unrealistic way to process life. Not to mention the abnormality in the need of "mentors" at his advanced age.

Does not mentally see or process that he is older. Thoughts regarding the 60 year old co-worker is emanating from his own self-preservation. This co-worker is his reflection (same age-range, unmarried status, and flirtatious mannerisms) so he glorifies this man to preserve his own delusional life.

Needs role-models so that he can mirror the behaviors he finds enviable...though this enviable behavior may be more appropriate for an immature and narcissistic twelve year old. Does not have a core-being or structure that guides his behaviors and forms his individual personality and identity; he mimics others.

No matter his age, believes to be at the prime of his life. Thinks he is in high school chasing the cheerleaders. (This actually worked for me during the honeymoon period. He saw me as young and hot. The bad side to this is he sees any woman who smiles at him as young and hot.)

He thinks he is Peter Pan and is forever seeking Tinker Bell.

14. **Exclusionary, Surrogate Partners:** Love-bombed me during the first few weeks but as the excitement of me wore off, I was emotionally and physically excluded in favor of others.

    Created an intimate date with his daughter doing something that I planned for us to do together. I arranged a Buddhist retreat for us but it never occurred because he was always "busy." One day, I received an exciting phone call that he was spending a day at the Buddhist retreat with his adult daughter. When I calmly shared my hurt over this, he responded, *You're jealous of my daughter* and he needed *alone time* with her.

    Codependency is familial. I bargained for hours for a gym membership so that we could work out together and when I stepped away to contemplate the terms, he gave my deal to his 30 year old daughter. He told me that she can't work out alone. They work out hours each day together and then go to lunch. The daughter still lives in her mother's house with her new husband.

    Adult children made into pseudo-lovers. Create dependent relationships to feel loved and needed.

    No sense of loyalty. I enjoy going out for coffee and when I didn't hear from him for days, he was taking female "friends" to my favorite coffee shop. When I mentioned my hurt, he told me that I was overreacting.

    Those with personality disorders create "Surrogate Partners" (this term used in the article *Narcissistic Love Triangles and Emotional Unavailability* by Fay Armitage) out of their adult children and female "friends" that they keep in their back-pocket for occasional ego-inflation, attention and stimulation.

This same article mentions that "Surrogate Partner" making is generational, whereas a parent subjected the child to being a Surrogate Partner and he in turns does this to his own child. This type of parent treats the child like a lover when they are on their "high" and discards them when they go into their "low."

Makes himself in *High-Demand* (term used in this same article) and manufactures insecurities and jealousies between people, i.e., triangulation. He creates exclusionary relationships because it is likely that when you approach him with concerns, he goes and smears you to his other sources. Because of his initial triangulation, he must keep people apart; he already made you look like a horrible person.

15. **Triangulating with Gaslighting:** Purposeful acts of keeping people apart to maintain control over all parties especially the insecure intimate partner. **Creating confusion.**

    Told me his female "friend" was happy for our relationship and yet he excluded me from all their gatherings. When I asked him where he was during these times, he lied. When I questioned him on the lie, he attacked me and accused me of being a horrible person and hating his female "friend." This threw my brain into confusion, I felt like a horrible and bad person (typical brain processing of an empath), and I lost focus of his lying.

    Creates uncomfortable feelings between people who don't know or talk with one another. Tells other party a different version of the problem he created between us. Did not tell female "friend" about his lying but instead told her that I was "jealous."

    Gaslighting is a low-level and primitive manipulation skill that a damaged and undeveloped person uses to manage their environment: the turning around of the events of an occurrence or story to inaccurately represent reality and to portray himself in a positive light.

According to Wikipedia, Gaslighting is, "a form of mental abuse in which information is twisted/spun, selectively omitted to favor the abuser, or false information is presented with the intent of making victims doubt their own memory, perception and sanity."

16. Functions Mostly on a Visual Level; Poor Auditory and Comprehension Skills:

Claims to be an aesthete or a person skilled in recognizing beauty. I was flattered and believed myself to be his Aesthetic Goddess.

Favorite yoga teacher was a man that grunted, "Look, Do!" When I tried to gently talk him through the correct building of a pose, he became frustrated.

Sees Soul-Connection when someone smiles at him and his mind transforms this smiley-person to an amazing beauty.

Believes he only attracts and is worthy of Perfection. Believed my "beauty and radiation" was a worthy match to his manly perfection (though he fluctuates between feeling grandiose and intense insecurity).

Saw himself in my adoring reflection and illumination upon him; I was his temporary self-confidence. When I held him accountable for a lie or an act that harmed me, he immediately turned away from me and sought another *glowing* reflection.

Searches facial expressions for acceptance. Desperate need for approval. Finding worth through others.

If this intense looking at our facial expressions and features (as if focusing on our words) comes later in the relationship, or after some trouble occurred and we called him out on it, this is the finding fault in our physical appearance and even in our character. We become ugly. This is The Devalue and Discard where we are knocked off the pedestal and we are transmuting, in his brain, into undesirable.

Superficial, shallow, and surface presentation only. Little ability to concentrate and contemplate on our conversations unless I was feeding his ego or revealing something sexual or trauma related from my past.

Undeveloped mental and emotional processing skills. Retained little about my life and confused most everything I told him.

The lack of comprehension skills, or the inability to focus, looks like sinister and deliberate gaslighting. Is gaslighting the motive, or is he so brain-damaged that gaslighting is ingrained in his interactive brain pattern?

I have no doubt that some very dangerous personalities use gaslighting as a deliberate method to control, but it should also be considered that damaged brains use gaslighting as a conditioned response to communicate in a world that they cannot manage through honesty, integrity, character, delayed gratification, and right motives.

17. **Lacks Focus and Follow-Through:** Brimming with ideas but does not have cognitive ability to organize or structure anything for completion.

Magical Thinking: Started writing a play twelve years ago, only persisted for a short time and only developed a few rough snippets. Now, refers to himself as a Play-write. He is going on

70 years old, does no work toward future achievement, and yet he believes that he will be famous.

Everything is rushed and sloppy. Little patience for details and no thinking through steps or systematically working through procedures. Proponent of *The Devil is in the Details.*

Brain is undisciplined and chaotic with the constant and obsessive need for highly stimulating distractions (people, activities).

May be able to work more slowly and deliberately if there is an ego-source observing or aiding him.

Low-level and skill job and needs to constantly flirt with women and interact with people while performing duties. Cannot handle responsibility.

Instant Gratification. Went a couple of years to college and only talked about the study groups he was in. He arrived early for class one day, picked up a non-textbook to read, fell so in love with this book that he had to drop out of college to finish reading it.

Many fly-by-night interests and these depend upon interests of current sexual partner. Took out many mortgages on homes with various wives and borrowed money from many people for business ventures. Ventures failed, homes went into default and loans were never paid back (No.9, Financial Problems).

A Boy And His Bipolar Mother

His brain was formed to survive under the stressful conditions of a child loved and given excessive and boyfriend-like attention by a mother, then this same mother, in an instant, retreats into her darkened bedroom, into herself, cruelly discarding her little boyfriend. She uses her little lover for her own high-gratification and for her compulsive need for external stimulation...to selfishly feed her own inner-frenzy. When her low-level sickness turns into morose stillness, she throws away the little boy's heart addicted to boundless doting. The little boy waits for his older girlfriend to emerge from her darkened bedroom to shower him once again with her overflowing love and attention: a cycle of limitless love given, cruelly aborted and anxiously anticipated. He is now an adult man, with the stunted emotional development of a little boy that lie in wait for his Great Lady Under the Earth who will be, once again, his beautiful Goddess of Love and Fertility. He must now operate in a grown-up world with grown-up minds.

This lapse in judgement taught me to control my time by organizing the events of my day for increased effectiveness. This means excluding people or events that are not arranged opportunities for organized effort that lead to self-growth. I was riding a man's wave (again) and losing sight of my own shore that included the treatment that I was worth and the working toward my own dreams. I was finally beached and forced into self-initiated moves.

Time is a sequence of events of your own choosing for stagnation, decline or growth. You must use time as an art, masterfully created, for your soul expression and expansion. When you control time, or the people and events you place in your day, and stop riding waves, you've mastered the universe.

The directional Will employs time correctly (Bailey, *Education In The New Age*, 77).

TWENTY-TWO

KNOW YOUR PATTERN AND CREATE A PLAN

When we are recovering from a sociopath or narcissist relationship and evaluating our participation in it, we should take this time to look into the pattern of our own life. Many of us will discover that our history consist of relationships of unequal footing or where there was a power discrepancy not in our favor. Abusers target those that are in a weak or transitioning period in their life, whether it be financial, educational, emotional, physical or those in a perpetually weak state from a chronic condition or childhood trauma.

My mother lives her life in automatic-mode of the least resistance to allow her life to be carried downstream instead of thinking realistically to forcefully move herself away from the wild current. She lives in a watery sea of emotions. Her dismissing reality validates her life of no effort and allowing herself to be carried along another person's flow. This is what led to her acquiescing to the destruction of her children. In addition to her not bonding with her own children, she is completely disconnected from her actions and her ability to make concerted movements that will lead to long-term wellness for herself and her offspring.

I am trying to get my mother's emotionalism out of me but still find myself unconsciously falling for the same emotionally detached and controlling men. This comes from my fear of the unknown world of true and unconditional love. I do not know how to attract a steady and loving relationship. I love in so far as my heart can stretch within constrained borders and in the knowing full well the man is destructive:

My Love Pattern:

✗ I fall in love with any man that showers me with attention, even though he is not my compatible match

✗ I realize he is not safe, nor is he right for me

✗ I do not leave when there is an early and easy out

✗ I communicate with him regarding my concerns

✗ He tells me words that I want to hear

✗ I feel love

✗ His words do not match his actions

✗ I communicate with him regarding my concerns; employ "teaching lessons"

✗ He is cold and unresponsive

✗ I retreat to safety, distance my physical and emotional self from him

✗ I yield in his presence and under his attention

✗ I feel love

✗ I see his true nature, again, in that he is not loyal or trustworthy

✗ I communicate with him regarding my concerns; employ "teaching lessons"

✗ He repeats meaningless words

✗ I hear words of hope that he does not speak

✗ I feel hope for his enlightenment, instead of my own enlightenment in walking away

✗ I diminish in respect as he grows stronger

✗ Pattern repeats

A person can only be reached at his own level and only to the extent of his capacity. A prophet who keeps preaching the word to a rock is undoubtedly a lunatic (Szepes, 273).

The Observer In The Field

Recognizing our patterns is a major step in healing. We can take notice of our own behavior by using The Observer In The Field approach. It is important that we act as *Observers* to watch ourselves in a *Field* as interactions and events unfold around us. How are others seeing us? How do others emotionally react in our presence? What are our common dramas? We can expand this observation out into the *field of our past* and notice patterns of reactions and non-reactions that surround our existence. As an Intelligent Observer, we are removed from the self-preserving ego and our sense of righteousness and can better see the emotional environment that entangles us. Instead of being the Emotional Player, we can then see ourselves from a different perspective and from there, learn and practice different behaviors. This is likely doing the opposite of your automatic programming.

Wisdom is the key to growth and exiting patterns or the cycle of death. People who are wise can access their spiritual cord connection and link to it when things go adrift; Narcissists cannot. He is unlinked...no spiritual cord that connects him higher nor that grounds him...it was cut off during childhood, or in some cases, not present at birth. He lacks higher purpose and does not see cause and effect. We are here on Earth, in this school, to keep going through the same lessons until we get it right. I can't tell you how many times I've gone through the Bad-Man Lesson, and in particular, The Old, Bad-Man Lesson, but each time, the harm they cause is less, and the understanding of who I am is more. I do not want to return here any longer to go through another life of Old, Bad-Man Lessons...hopefully, I will stop returning all together to this treacherous planet where its people, animals and nature are destroyed and my soul will be allowed to move forward ...untrapped.

Let The Sociopath move on to another trap of chaos, dysfunction, hatred and overall devastation. We are free.

Seeing your life pattern does not mean that you are going to snap out of it. Those of us that repeat bad patterns do so on an instinctual level. Instinctual thinking and the resulting behaviors are the attributes of the lowest level of consciousness. We need to develop our instinct into intelligence and our intelligence into intuition. This is done by seeing the energy that creates the circumstances and events that surround us. An intelligent breakdown of our instinctual pattern must not only be processed through, but we must learn to use intuition to spot when this pattern creeps into our lives....despite our emotional connection to its familiarity. An intelligent analysis of our instinctual life pattern does no good unless we change our interaction when it appears in our environment. We must learn to nip it in the bud!

Change The Response To Your Pattern

All that is needed is to access the dominant experiences in your life. Your patterns will not instantly disappear, but you will learn to see it when it enters your life. You can then improve your response to it by being mentally proactive instead of emotionally reactive. Respond to your pattern with care, deliberation and quality. This pro-action takes practice. Your motivation for corrective action comes from being struck down by this pattern so many times that you are finally fed up with your present condition.

Divine Discontent is being so sick and tired of your life that you either change or you disintegrate. Indeed, it can be a great thing if you choose the former and recreate your life. Some people need to hit rock bottom to use Divine Discontent for their renewal. Other people use it while still adequately surviving but they are consumed with a sense of unease and dissatisfaction. The more you are negatively affected by a bad pattern, the more chances you have to respond to crises in quality ways. The people who never adjust their response apparatus, or never make effort for improvement, are the weak souls (narcissists, sociopaths, apaths, the mentally or physically sick). The world is filled with these people! The more crises a person experiences, the more chances to become a more quality responder and therefore, a more evolved and wise human.

Apparent barriers to progress are only spurs to renewed endeavour and thus seeking to "lead him out" from any limiting condition (Bailey, Education in the New Age, 83).

Growth is learning to respond to your environment in more constructive ways!

1. **Realize the instinctive, lower-drive behind what you pursue and create.**

   I am attracted to older men because I think they will protect me. I am looking for a parent. I am tired of taking care of myself. I am looking for my soul mate.

2. **Put your realization into an intellectual meaning.**

   All my experiences have been that older men who have a long history of partner jumping, and who seek much younger women for intimate relationships, have serious personality and/or psychological issues. I have never been safe, cherished or taken care of by this type of man. I've always taken care of myself better than any man has done thus far. Men have created confusion, chaos, and destruction in my life.

3. **Create a plan to reverse your instinctive patterns.** "Reversing" is the key word. Do the opposite of what you've always done.

   I will focus on higher goals and not a man. I will maintain my boundaries and routines to achieve goals and will not put my dreams aside for anyone. I will create my own safe and nourishing environment. I will continue to take care of myself in the greatest way possible and with renewed strength and creativity. I will not be consumed by a man who penetrates my life. I will take things slowly and deliberately with not only men, but with anyone that enters my life. (I laugh when thinking about doing the opposite of our instinctual patterns: the *Seinfeld* episode where George does everything the opposite of his normal inclinations and his life turns around for the better!)

4. **Use intuition to *see* and understand when you are trying to bring back the old pattern.** Reverting to an old pattern is done to achieve a sense of familiarity and comfort and to avoid the effort required for change. *See* into what you are manifesting in not only yourself, but in your environment. This is done by feeling the good or bad energy in everything you do.

I feel nervous and stressed out when with Mr.Oh because I know, in a short time, he will create confusion in our relationship by lying, disappearing, or excluding me. He does this every time we get close. I feel good energy when I am safe at home learning, working on my dreams, eating healthy foods and loving all the animals that surround me.

Inertia is easy and it is what most people fall into. Movement is required and must be initiated. Moving in Grace is something to strive for.

"Psychological change requires resisting unproductive automatic reflexes and consciously and willfully choosing other alternatives - choices that are different, even opposite, from the automatic reflex - sometimes these new ways of behaving are frightening, but they hopefully are more efficient ways of coping" (Kreisman & Straus, 90).

Good Practices When Meeting Someone New:

1. Take things slowly and deliberately.

2. Keep your smart phone and electronic devices private.

3. Do not reveal intimate details about other partners, especially the sexual component (this is only to incite jealousy and competition anyway).

4. Do not immediately reveal insecurities or too much information about childhood and parents (if unpleasant, can be used against you and to keep you in an inferior position).

5. Do not excessively see, talk with or text the new person. This shows as neediness (can indicate your own inner-desperation, compulsion, addiction to attention).

6. *Do not sleep with someone right away. Even non-sociopaths obtain emotional, psychological, and physical highs during the honeymoon period.

7. **Do not be provoked into emotional reactions.

8. Stay true to your dreams. Strive toward a balance of pursuing your calling and interacting in moderation and with boundaries in healthy relationships.

*Do not become physically intimate with someone too quickly because the combination of the emotional and physical bond is a more intensified, entwined spiritual one and therefore, harder to unwind from. And if someone creates an atmosphere that leads to a quick emotional attachment, this may be the sign of a person with a personality/mental disorder that is only interested in quickly winning you over so that your returned attention and admiration will feed his ego.

**When I fall into negative emotional feelings, I access my intellectual plane to see if it is me that's being too sensitive or the person is purposefully creating insecurities and an unsafe environment for me and our relationship. This is The Observer In The Field approach. Stand back and watch yourself as if you are another person. My emotionalism manifests as a record spinning out-of-control in my head and I start seeing everything this person does as a personal violation. If it is my own drama creation, I will take a time-out, not mention my concerns, and do a wait-and-see. Things always unfold naturally. If I determine the other person is cluttering up our relationship with confusion, I know that I need to leave this atmosphere.

Create a strong and soul-nourishing routine to your life to minimize and/or prevent pitfalls.

Here Is Part Of My Routine:

- ✔ Read high-level philosophical materials each morning to improve the workings of my mind and soul.

- ✔ Reflect on the lessons transmitted and try to incorporate these in my writings.

- ✔ Write for as long as possible until other duties are necessary.

- ✔ Study a new math lesson to impart on my evening math students. This improves my mind skills and repairs mental and brain damage that occurred as a result of childhood abuse, the resulting trauma and a history of unhealthy relationships. The math lessons that I study are one-step above my current ability and comfort zone.

- ✔ Moderate exercise (yoga, walk my dogs, weights).

- ✔ Return home in the evening to retreat into quietness, or to read, or to watch a science, math or soul development video.

You cannot eliminate something, you must substitute for it instead.

If we establish good and healthy routines that improve our mind, body and soul, we can bypass some obstacles that may creep in. My routine saved me from allowing Mr.Oh to absorb me.

Creative work is not sporadic. It is trained attention. This is genius.

In order to put people into a proper cognitive organization (perspective), you must keep your nose to the grindstone, or pursue your own passions, through creative expressions, projects, service work. When you are focused on your own work, your work for the environment and the world at large, then a new 'love' will not become your laser-beam focus and you can shelve this person in a way that will not be all consuming. When we set structured time aside for ourselves and our own soul work, it is hard for outside forces to penetrate our entire existence. It is when we are uncertain and not dedicated about our soul work that other people can take us along for an emotional ride. (Soul work is the mission we are supposed to be on for this incarnation. We know what it is but we find excuses and distractions to not follow it.)

Recognize when you are operating low-level with a person. There will be nothing going on as far as higher goals, your physical, emotional and mental bodies will be weak, and you will feel anxious.

It is okay to have time set aside for less focused work, but organize this time after you work on your main and important task for growth. Operating from intelligence, I understand my natural rhythm and that I get tired and want to retreat when the sun sets, therefore, I go to bed early and get up early to do my reading and writing. This ensures that if a distraction comes my way in the middle part of the day, I can go for that coffee with someone that may not be my perfect counterpart, knowing full well that I am still on my mission.

It takes a crisis (or crises) to wake up and to not live in a disconnect from who we are and where we are going as souls. I am recreating myself and I am growing up. As I travel through my recovery and healing process from a lifetime of confusion, and succumbing to the final and most insane Sociopath, I realize that I am finally blooming. I am growing up in the sense that I realize that I was always guided by my old soul but I was using naivety to *connect* with people believing they too had my same innate and advanced sense of fair treatment instilled within them. Old souls want to lead gently, but unfortunately this makes us prime targets for predators. Being an Empath does not mean being gullible, and it certainly does not mean living carelessly in a world of predators.

We need to work hard to kick-start our new life of realizations and learn to react differently to our surroundings: remove ourselves from engaging in continual emotional situations and instead, use our intellect to soar. We can change our automatic habits by creating new habits, or deliberately changing our ingrained responses. I practice not emotionally reacting to the bad people that I tend to attract, but remain calm and intellectually observe their internal and external energies that they surround me with. I now stand back as an Observer; it's fascinating. Stabilize emotional reactions and radiate out more brilliantly using intellect. We grow up and evolve; Sociopaths only grow old.

Growth is not taking straight and even steps upward but the navigating of a spiral staircase. We wind backward, see where we've been, and then inch ourselves forward and higher with a renewed perspective on what was, and what needs to be done as a result.

Growing Intuition

Intuition grows by practicing deductive reasoning or applying general theories to specific observations. It is a mind exercise developed by focusing on our surroundings and looking for patterns: manifesting wisdom. Intuition is the extension of our ordinary senses and consciousness. It is being an acute observer. *Disturbed men ruin women by absorbing and controlling them; unhealthy women are ruined by allowing themselves to be absorbed and controlled by disturbed men. Men that absorb and control me, ruin me. If Mr. Blank absorbs me, taking control of my physical, emotional, mental existence, and I allow it, I am not only attracting another disturbed man, but I am operating in an unhealthy way and I will be ruined.*

Learning Wisdom is an outgrowth of knowledge and of grasping understandingly the meaning which lies behind the outer imparted facts. It is the power to apply knowledge in such a manner that sane living and an understanding point of view, plus an intelligent technique of conduct, are the natural results (Bailey, *Education In The New Age*, 82).

Intuition Is Approached By Going From:

- Whole to the Part
- Periphery to the Center
- Universal to the Particulars

I experienced an unexpected intuitive blast and it came as a loud voice in my car. I was driving past Mr.Oh's and my favorite quirky fast-food restaurant and a voice shook me alert and said, "Go in, you will know the truth." I ignored the voice because I don't believe in voices and plus, I didn't want to know the truth. The Voice spoke these words again. I rationalized and I fought against turning my steering wheel left into that restaurant: *If he cannot be trusted, and I must check up on him, then, I should not be with him.* I then realized that truth is good and should always be pursued because it prevents living a life of confusion and delusion. I pulled into the restaurant.

There he was, there she was...walking merrily into *Our Place.* I followed and stood behind them in line at the counter. She was mirroring me by standing one step behind him as he *charmingly* ordered her food...the same food he orders for me. **We are ALL *Interchangeable People-Parts* to the personality disordered.** She turned around, looked at me and meekly smiled. Just like something I would do...Narcissists and their codependent Empaths!

Mr.Oh turned around, saw me, a quiver shimmied up his spine, he turned blank and casually said, "Oh, Hi Lynna." Ignoring him, I turned to her and calmly stated that she was with a cheating, lying man that obsessively chases attention. They both stared at me and then walked outside to sit down on the patio. I calmly walked up to the counter and the guy with the smiley face took my order: "I'll have two of what he ordered her." I took their tray when it came ready, and with confidence, meandered it outside, placed it gently down between the two and with the dignity of an Empath Goddess, told her to "Get Self-Esteem." I glided away to get my food and then to drive away like a graceful ballroom dancer on wheels: An Empath Rising.

As far as the voice of My Helper goes, it was my Intuition knocking on the door of my life. I knew the general themes of Mr.Oh's poor character: his neurotically bored personality, his obsessive hunting for attention and adoration, his inability to ever be alone, his *Need to be Needed,* and his compulsive flirting nature. I then applied this to a specific situation that I happened to be driving past and came to a logical and specific conclusion: It was Mr.Oh's lunch hour, *Our* restaurant was across the street from where he works, and I understood that he cannot eat alone. Feeding people is his manipulative, not to mention effective, tool that he neurotically employs to tap into most anyone's need for caretaking and a free lunch (it worked with me): Instant Ego-Supply. I made generalizations about Mr.Oh and realized his patterns, and then made a narrow or specific guess by steering into that restaurant at the perfect moment. The loud voice in my car was my inner fears leading me toward outer strength...My Helper.

Developing Intuition is the Practice of Synthesizing our Environment.

The capacity to move forward (as life unfolds) into that world of meaning which underlies the world of outer phenomena and begin to view human happenings in terms of the deeper spiritual and universal values (Bailey, *Education In The New Age,* 82).

Narcissists create stressful environments and this leads to our physical, emotional and mental problems, and as a result, we shut down from our intuition...from ourselves. Think about yourself when you are with a Narcissist: You have diminished energy and shrink in stress because you live in fear of his lying, flirting, cheating, betraying and disloyal personality. You live in jealousy, obsessiveness, possessiveness...in anxiety. You know you are interchangeable, replaceable, disposable and no soul can survive, let alone thrive, under these circumstances. Every woman who looks at him becomes suspect and you are consumed with suspicion and fear that he found someone new when you are not with him.

Enter The World Of Ideas:

1. Register Impressions (ideas, meanings, purposes)

2. Develop these Impressions into Thought Forms

3. Bring these Thought Forms to Conscious Awareness

4. Energize your Conscious Awareness to move toward a good situation or away from an unhealthy one.

Keep a diary of extensions in sense-consciousness that you assume to be speculative or abstract and of no real significance...not trivial events but serendipitous moments. Synthesize the concrete world of material form with the abstract world of meaning. We must be sensitive to intuition that will enable us to distinguish between the real and unreal. Reveal yourself and your sensitivity on paper. Watch as your intuition grows.

I then intuitively saw the inner emotional workings of the women who surround men with personality disorders: Apath and codependent women support Narcissists on the sidelines as his Empath girlfriends are slowly destroyed. This is The Sociopath, Apath, Empath Triangle. We all have our roles to play in this sad social circle and because a Narcissist people-pleases, he is able to keep a network of women "friends" protecting him when he becomes "victim" to another "bad ex." However, it is the people-pleasing nature of The Socio/Narc that initially won our hearts. But how his people-pleasing bites us back when we are the intimate target being destroyed...he has a network of supporters! My *vision* was clear and it was accurate. I opened up the workings of my brain and I realized that emotionally and mentally stunted people dance together in their own made-up delusional dream to survive this lifetime; to survive with the least amount of effort.

Develop your Intuition by transforming your positive tendencies into habits. Make these habits a part of your daily rhythm.

My tendency is to think and talk about the inner-workings of people and the world. This tendency evolved into the constant learning of philosophical and spiritual matters and synthesizing my learnings in the written form to help myself and others. This is all done to control the forces in my environment so these forces can no longer control me. As a result, intuition can come into play.

TWENTY-THREE

THE RETURN OF MY SOCIOPATH

I thought I was immune from My Sociopath's continuing smear-campaign, lies, isolation tactics...I thought I was safe because I wrote about sociopath abuse on the internet. No one is insane enough to try to continually ruin someone who writes about his harmful and destructive behaviors. How can an old man, that appears creepy, get away with crying the victim his entire life, when he's had nothing but corpses of destruction in his past? Our divorce decree even says: *To not disrupt my right to peaceful enjoyment of living.*

There is a debate in the world of sociopath and narcissist writers whether to expose Narcissists and the harm they cause (even when concealing their names). Most say that it creates an even more dangerous situation for the writer (perhaps true in cases of psychopaths). I can assure you, it does not matter what we do, or what we do not do...they keep us forever chained to their cluster of demons. I can blame my writings for My Sociopath's continuing attempts to ruin me, but advocacy to spread sociopath awareness is not to blame. When I was with My Sociopath, he was ruining all the other women that he ever entangled with. His expression was sorrowful and full of dread as he told crowds of people that his daughter was an internet prostitute because of her horrible mother. The daughter was a typical California bikini model. Both daughter and ex-wife were not exposing him, but in fact, hiding out from him; the daughter even changed her name to separate herself from him. The last girlfriend was the epitome of a low self-esteemed, enabler who was a mothering, care-taker and always desperate for a man, any man; she was nothing short of a wet-nurse for the spoiled brat that screamed and grabbed for constant stimulation. This girlfriend paid My Sociopath's bills as he lazily hung around his failing business all day, gossiping with people that brought in no business, and lurking the internet for attention and admiration. Yet, he left her for me, and proceeded to destroy what was left of her shattered-self through his non-stop gossip, half-truths and his sorrowful moans regarding her defects. She too hid away from the falling discard rubble; from the smear-campaign rabble.

The Sociopath must win at all cost...to see you completely ruined because his twisted soul believes he is your only life-source...that you must stay forever encased in the hell-chamber that he resides in. He took control of you in the honeymoon period and this is when he slithered inside your soul to settle for eternity. We saw his manic possessing of every cell of our being when still with him: when we focused on something other than him, he created drama so that we would wildly react back in his direction to only tighten our own chains back onto him.

Since he never feels real joy and freedom, neither should you. Your renewed smile and optimism means that he lost control of your body, mind and emotions...you are thriving, authentic and genuine. He knows that he is trapped in another temporary honeymoon period with another temporary target that is already letting him down, and because he cannot feel safe and settled, neither should you. Your thriving means that you are not as bad as what he bellowed out to his comrades that you are. You are going against the mangled image that he created of you. When he absorbed your light, he wanted your Will. Will is the spark, or drive, that you access to grow and evolve outside him...in the face of what he did to you. Nothing irritates a Sociopath more than a former target with Will.

The Sociopath keeps returning to his same supporters year after year to ensure that you remain bad in their eyes. He does this by changing the timeline. My Sociopath bought a property with Karen when we were married. I was talked into relinquishing my rights to this property during our divorce. This issue had been long ago dismissed. Three years later after I moved on, and he ran out of lust from his most recent honeymoon period, he frantically ran to Karen's home, pounded on her door and explained that I was coming after her property. If he is not reversing history, he outright lies and blames you for his current struggles. Three-years later and my being far away in mind and body, he is telling everyone that I am hurting his business. His business was failing 20-years before I came along.

A Sociopath keeps an Enemy Effigy of you burning in order to keep his entourage train following him on his everlasting victimization ride. Real victims of abuse are shame-filled and blame themselves for the position that they believe they got themselves into. They do not make continual announcements of continual abuse by long ago exes.

By keeping me paddling upstream to try to keep everything afloat in my life, he believes that he is effortlessly drifting downstream. However, Sociopaths are rash and unthinking decision makers and their past collateral damage always catches up to them and collides with their current life of drama. Sociopaths never find peace...it is their karma to suffer through this life because of the suffering they cause. People who make bad decisions along their way can find redemption when they realize they caused suffering, apologize and try to make amends. Sociopaths do not do this.

The Western idea of Karma is distorted: Karma is not a bad, scary and elusive concept and it does not have to wait for many lifetimes to unfold. Karma, good or bad, is made in each moment...by what we do, say and think. We can create good karma right now by choosing to do even the simplest of things: Cleaning house leads to better energy and perhaps feeling more comfortable in inviting a neighbor over...a neighbor that may turn out to be a good friend and someone to go to in need. We can create good karma in more profound ways by doing service work. The opposite, or bad karma, can be created in a moment by reacting to a mean person who may turn around and violently harm us. He then may go home to lash out against his family and pets. The cycle never ends: he may have been abused by his parents and his parents abused by his grandparents. His children will enter into the world of adults.

Sociopaths encompass the lowest level of incarnated souls. They function on the low physical plane: pursue food, shelter, material items and sex. They operate on the low emotional level: seek attention, adoration, glamour and popularity. Sociopaths live their entire lives in a fight with the hell they create on earth. They are chained to and tortured by their monstrous emotional enemies: subjugation, control, manipulation and the dependency on weak people to fulfill their ego needs.

I was bound body and soul to the morgue of this world by handcuffs of desire and selfishness (Szepes, 87).

Sociopaths occupy a lower place in the world of souls than those entities in the Animal, Plant and Mineral Kingdoms. Spiders are spectacularly brilliant as they weave webs and unlike Sociopaths, they never trap themselves in their own web. A Lotus grows in mud and opens its heart center to shine onto the world. Sociopaths never grow out of their murky nature; they never learn to operate heart center, but stir from their lower sacral region, and thus, stay stuck in a dark womb. Coal transforms to diamonds that radiate yellow-sparkle sunbeams from multiple facets. Sociopaths are one-dimensional and never illuminate into the world.

My Sociopath is telling everyone that he is *Going to War* with me, that he is *In Battle*. Yet, he hangs out across the street from where I live (against court orders), telling tales about me as he points toward my home. He is trying to purchase a home two doors down from me. When I was with him, he wanted to buy the house for sale next door to his ex-wife and daughter. He is only *alive* when in control of past and current targets. My Sociopath fights his own demons as his facebook quote explains: *Life is a battle, enter it armed.*

He must force his physical presence into my surroundings so that I am reminded of his existence. He fears that if he is out of my mind … then he does not exist.

You can live in freedom by walking steady and self-assured away from your previous life filled with hurt and trauma and instead enter a new life of endless possibilities. This takes the death of the old you and the ceasing of repetitive behavioral, thinking and emotional patterns that keep you tied to monsters. A Sociopath stays forever encrusted in his own tomb...we do not have to stay encased inside his burial chamber...we can emerge, evolve and enthrall.

Live Free and Let your Soul Lead: Keep a healthy physical body, steady emotions and high thoughts. We return to glowing beauty, health, and vitality when we free ourselves from unhealthy physical, emotional and mental attachments.

Revitalize Your Body, Refocus Your Emotions, Restore Your Mind, and Realign Your Soul.

- Eliminate fear.

- Work on your dreams each day (a little or a lot).

- Keep Learning.

- Do Service Work.

- Stand steady and firm no matter what occurs.

- Apply common-sense to all matters. Synthesize your environment into accurate meanings.

- Use careful and controlled speech.

- Sleep much. The hours from 10 pm to 6 am are the best.

- Keep busy but do not overtire the body.

- Exercise lightly.

- Eat healthy and enjoyable foods.

- Use the sun for energy and healing.

- Relax, have fun, so that you may be rid of tension and start fresh again.

Though your feet may be in mud, keep your head held high toward the sun.

POSTSCRIPT

I started this writing adventure more than two years ago. I do not have writing degrees so not only was this an evolution of my soul, but of trying to grow myself into a writer. This was a challenge on a vast number of levels. I sometimes write in passive voice but after much fighting with myself, I came to realize, it is okay to break away from the dictates of others and to be free...to be me...in whatever voice that may be.

During the writing of this book, I was rear ended by an uninsured driver, on a suspended license and who was talking on his cell phone. My car was totaled and I was sent to the hospital with a severe concussion. If this were not enough, I was diagnosed with Type 1 diabetes, formerly known as Juvenile Diabetes. Type 1 is an auto-immune disorder and is very different from Type 2, or the diet and lifestyle diabetes. It is rare to be diagnosed with Type 1 over the age of 20-years-old so the doctors did not suspect it whereby causing me to go undiagnosed for a very long time. As a result, heart and brain damage occurred.

It is mandatory, as a Type 1, to immediately go on insulin or death is the result. I declined insulin and have been trying to cure myself with a high protein, low carbohydrate, no sugar diet with the addition of my own self-created flow movement routines for healing and restoration. I have been successful longer than any known documented case of a Type 1 not taking insulin or medications.

Surviving life takes Will. Writing, editing, and converting this book on my own took Will. Will is focusing on one thing at a time. Will is not getting it right...sleeping on it and trying it again the next day with a new perspective. Will does not take being perfect...it just takes focusing on a worthy endeavor and chipping away at it with consistency...some days a little, some days a lot...one day not going far...another day going farther than ever expected.

Will is Doing. When you are in a state of Doing with Focus, you are in a state of moving away from obsessive thinking about what the sociopath did to you. And on a spiritual level...your spirit is moving far ahead in its evolution whereby leaving the sociopath's soul to continue its dreadful karmic pattern of repeating destructive relationship patterns. You are Healing...he is degenerating.

ABOUT THE AUTHOR

LYNNA KIVELA, MA

Lynna graduated from California State University, San Bernardino with a BA in the Social Sciences, from Chapman University in Orange, California with an MA in Special Education, and thereafter received her math teaching credential. She is also a certified yoga teacher and specializes in restorative, healing and trauma release movement routines. She still struggles in the keeping away of negative forces (creepy men; insane women) and in trying to keep herself on a higher mental plane instead of wallowing in low-level emotionalism (fear, insecurity, anxiety, guilt, self-loathing...). But the quest is worth it and she knows, most of the time, that healing isn't final; it is a process of passing through events (time), or the moment by moment movement upon the path of action, with clarity of vision, dignity, and within the aura of goodness and service...pushing one's evolution on...being directed by one's higher calling...being soul infused...realizing and then seeking one's Grand Destiny. She lives in Oceanside, California with her rescue animals that patiently, and with devotion, tolerate her quirky ways.

WORKS CITED

"Autism Spectrum Disorders." *A Parent's Guide to Symptoms and Diagnosis on the Autism Spectrum*. Web. 02 June 2015.

Armitage, Fay. "Narcissistic Love Triangles and Emotional Unavailability." *Examiner.com*. 08 Jan. 2014. Web. 24 Apr. 2015.

Bailey, Alice A. "THE MASTERS." *Letters On Occult Meditation*. 4th ed. New York: Lucis, 1939. Print.

Bailey, Alice. *Education in the New Age*. New York: Lucis Pub., 1954. Print.

Brother, An Elder. *Unsigned Letters from an Elder Brother*. London: Fowler, 1930. Print.

Eriksson, J. M., L. M. Andersen, and S. Bejerot. "Short Autism Screening Test." *Psych Central.com*. Web. 21 Apr. 2015.

"Gaslighting." *Wikipedia*. Wikimedia Foundation, Web. 24 Apr. 2015.

Hand Clow, Barbara. "Kundalini, Astrology, and the Key Life Transitions Barbara Hand Clow." YouTube, Web. 23 Feb. 2015.

Kreisman, Jerold J., and Hal Straus. *I Hate You, Don't Leave Me*: Perigee Group., 2010. Print.

Leinen, Linda. "Reflections on a Homeless Muse." *The Task at Hand*. WordPress, 17 July 2008. Web. 10 Apr. 2015.

Szepes, Mária. *The Red Lion: The Elixir of Eternal Life: An Alchemist Novel*. Yelm, WA: Horus Pub., 1997. 26. Print.